What people are

A Fairy Path

A Fairy Path is a unique look into the intersectionality of Romanian fairy belief, life outside the norm, and finding a place in a changing world, deftly interweaving the author's experiences and thoughts as she came of age in Communist Romania and reconciled her experiences with fairies against the unbelief of those around her. This is not your typical biography but rather works to guide the reader, along with the author's younger self, through the process of integrating personal experience, folk belief, and magic into a cohesive whole in a world that is too often hostile to those who are different. A fascinating and valuable read.

Morgan Daimler, author of *Aos Sidhe* and *Fairies: A Guide to the Celtic Fair Folk*

In *A Fairy Path: The Memoir of a Young Fairy Seer in Training*, Daniela Simina offers a beautifully written tale of a childhood full of fairy magic, yet lived in fear during in Romania's Communist past. It's a story based in truth, of traditional folk beliefs passed on from grandmother to granddaughter and practiced in secret for the good of the community. It's also about growing up, coming of age, and learning to take on the responsibilities of being a witch. The book ends with a wonderful collection of genuine charms and spells, as learnt by Daniela from her youngest days.

Lucya Starza, author of *Poppets and Magical Dolls* and *Scrying*

The question that plagues any work of autobiography is "how much?" For the author, how much to reveal, how much personal feeling to lay bare? For the reader, how much to believe? How far to trust the author's recollection, of their version of events? This is doubly true when the story recounts childhood memories. We are at our most vulnerable discussing our formative years, the precious memories and painful childish hurts. When our childhood deviates from the norm, it becomes an act of faith to allow others in, to offer secrets for outside eyes to judge. *A Fairy Path* is both a fascinating story of folk traditions surviving under the brutal fist of a communist regime and a deeply touching coming of age story. The wild, free and sometimes unruly ten-year-old at its heart battles to be her true self, while family life and school and friendship pull her in different directions. Her Grandmother is a respected local wise woman, whose path involves working with traditional Zâne (Fairies) and a burning desire to be part of that world fuels her rebellion, but also inspires her. I read this account of an unusual childhood with great enjoyment. The raw emotion of the child still rings true, decades after the events described. There is a simplicity to the retelling that engages and the description of traditional Romanian beliefs and practices, hidden beneath village life is gripping. Fear of officialdom is never far away, from the cruel Comrade teacher to the policemen interrogating a ten-year-old. For those interested in a fairy path, it offers valuable insight into both the rewards and perils of interacting with powerful entities. For anyone interested in folk traditions and beliefs it's a fascinating read and a touching childhood memoir.

Geraldine Moorkens Byrne, author of *The Caroline Jordan Mystery* series and *Dreams of Reality*

Over the past few years, there have been a number of excellent books published on the subject of fairies and fairy witchcraft. However, this is the first I've read that introduces the tradition through the child's eye view of someone growing up within that tradition and learning from a beloved elder. Daniela Simina's *A Fairy Path* is no simple memoir, though. This is the magic of storytelling when used to teach, and there is much to learn in these pages. The Romania that Daniela grew up in was one in which the magical practices and beliefs of her traditional culture were unacceptable to the governing regime. At turns, this account is dreamlike and wondrous. It opens a midnight door lit by lamplight and reveals a hidden Romania in which old women conspired to heal members of their community in secret, threw cards, and offered to Zâne. We see a child who couldn't imagine herself growing up to be anything other than one of those women, her desire to learn those ways, and her family's fear of discovery. Her grandmother's teachings and hard-won knowledge permeate each page. Though dreamlike, Daniela's writing is grounded by not only the harsh realities of living with such prejudice, but also the very real consequences of her magical mistakes. This book would be an invaluable addition to the library of anyone who is interested in fairies and fairy witchcraft.

Cat Heath, author of *Elves, Witches &Gods*, and *Essays from the Crossroads*

A Fairy Path

The Memoir of a Young Fairy Seer
in Training

A Fairy Path

The Memoir of a Young Fairy Seer
in Training

Daniela Simina

**MOON
BOOKS**

Winchester, UK
Washington, USA

JOHN HUNT PUBLISHING

First published by Moon Books, 2023
Moon Books is an imprint of John Hunt Publishing Ltd., No. 3 East Street, Alresford
Hampshire SO24 9EE, UK
office@jhpbooks.net
www.johnhuntpublishing.com
www.moon-books.net

For distributor details and how to order please visit the 'Ordering' section on our website.

ISBN: 978 1 80341 402 7
978 1 80341 403 4 (ebook)
Library of Congress Control Number: 2022945627

A CIP catalogue record for this book is available from the British Library.

Design: Lapiz Digital Services

UK: Printed and bound by CPI Group (UK) Ltd, Croydon, CR0 4YY
Printed in North America by CPI GPS partners

We operate a distinctive and ethical publishing philosophy in
all areas of our business, from our global network of authors to
production and worldwide distribution.

Contents

To Grandma

A Note from the Author

I shall begin by saying that the story you are about to read is not a work of fiction, and the word memoir in the title does actually reference my own experience as an apprentice to a fairy seer, my grandmother. This is an autobiographical work, and everything in this book is recorded as accurately as possible.

Aside from explicitly mentioning the country, Romania, where the events described take place, no other specific location is named. To protect the privacy of the protagonists, albeit none of them still being alive at the time the book was written, all the names – except my own – have been changed. In order to preserve the authentic flavor and give an accurate sense of the time, place, and the culture where the events take place, I chose to use Romanian names instead of anglicized versions.

The charms and spells recorded here are those I learned from my grandmother, and I did my best to reproduce them as accurately as possible, which has its own challenges, considering that some expressions are specific to the Romanian language and do not have English equivalents. Also, I do not pretend to assume the position of cultural ambassador, nor do I speak on behalf of any fairy seer within Romanian culture other than myself. As the reader will understand, such practices were solitary par excellence. Consequently, the likelihood of the same charm circulating as countless variations is high, and it is beyond the scope of this book to analyze commonalities and differences in fairy-related practices across various regions of Romania.

A Fairy Path: The Memoir of a Young Fairy Seer in Training introduces the reader to the world of fairy witchcraft, as experienced through the eyes of a child who grows straddling two overlapping yet conflicting realities: one represented by the living tradition of fairy seers and medicine women in Romania, and the other one shaped by life in a society governed by a dictatorial regime.

A Fairy Path has also been written with the desire to offer those walking a fairy-led path some material to work with. I believe that one does not have to be Romanian or of Romanian descent by any degree to connect with fairy seership as practiced in that part of the world. Fairies, same as gods, call whoever they please. To this avail, the book explicitly details charms and spells for those interested to adapt and use. Appendix 1 is a partial reconstruction of *Daniela's Little Book of Magic*, a magical journal that I kept as a child. The spells and charms recorded there, while informed by what my training was at the time, can be adapted to fit any type of practice. Appendix 2 provides a list of resources for those interested to understand better the broader context for Romanian fairy traditions.

Now take a breath and relax. Allow yourself to slip a few decades back in time to a place cradled between the Carpathian Mountains and the Danube River, and follow a child's journey into fairy seership.

Daniela Simina
July, 2022

Chapter 1

"There's no such thing as Santa!"

The hand tightened its grip on my shoulder. It hurt, but I didn't say anything. Then, the teacher pushed me away with the disgust one would push away something dirty.

"Time out", she yelled, her arm stretched out stiffly and her index finger pointing like a spearhead to the corner of the classroom. I felt my knees and stomach trembling in a mix of anxiety, sadness, and indignation. I walked away slowly and turned to face the wall.

Muttering something about talking to my parents, the teacher stormed out, leaving both the class and the new assistant astonished. We all had seen Comrade[1] Caran getting angry before, but this topped off everything we had ever witnessed.

From the corner of my eye, I could see the window and catch a glimpse of the gray clouds hanging low. I could feel the snow coming. Thinking of snowflakes made me smile despite the whole situation. Just then, the classroom door swung open and Comrade Caran burst in. Her eyes fell on me.

"What is so entertaining?" I kept silent. "I asked you a question, and I expect an answer." She sounded quite calm, but there was something in the way she spoke that made me think of the thunder roll heard from afar and forecasting the impending storm.

"I can feel snow coming, Comrade." I kept my voice as neutral as I could and tried my best to sound respectful.

Comrade Caran jumped, as if the chair she barely sat on had suddenly caught on fire. "You cannot feel the snow coming! You can think of snow coming; or you may wish for it, but don't you EVER dare to tell us that you can feel the snow coming!" Her face contorted as she yelled. The teacher went on shouting, her voice already shrill, climbing yet another octave.

"And for your information, the weather forecast doesn't mention any snow for today or tomorrow. I'll meet your parents during recess. We need to figure out what's wrong with you. Two weeks ago, you tried to make us believe that your cat glows green and blue. This morning you burst into the classroom sharing about an encounter you had with Santa Claus, and now you are telling us that you can feel the snow coming? You live in the twentieth century, in glorious Communist times, not in a fairy tale. WAKE UP!"

As if screaming wasn't enough, Comrade Caran furiously slammed her hand against the desk to underline her last words. To my greatest satisfaction, I saw her palms springing together quickly, her left hand massaging the right one which she obviously hurt when hitting the hard surface.

There was silence. I hung my head low, hoping that nobody would see that I turned scarlet. Minutes went by. Suddenly, the assistant teacher's voice broke the silence. "Comrade Caran, should the children get dressed and go out for recess? It's, um... snowing." I sighed and hardly contained a smile. The bell rang. The sound couldn't have come soon enough. Comrade Caran turned toward me.

"You'll spend the recess in detention. I phoned you parents, and I'll meet both your mother and father in my office." In my heart, the faint glimmer of a smile died out.

The first snow of the year was too important an event, so no one paid attention to me anymore. I stood by the window watching the snowflakes dance through the air. I pressed my forehead against the glass.

"So, if I could see colors around my cat that no one else seems to see, if I really can feel snow coming, does it mean that the man I saw this morning was Santa? But if there's no such thing as Santa, then who did I see?"

Father picked me up from school as he often did in wintertime. He didn't break the silence until we got home. It wasn't only until after I had lunch that he finally addressed me.

"And where was Santa standing when you saw him this morning?" Father asked as we stood by the kitchen window looking outside. He spoke in a matter-of-fact tone, and I could tell that he had no intention to make fun of me. I pointed to a spot in the backyard. "Let's go take a closer look," he said.

We walked outside. Father stared intently at my room's window on the second floor. I followed his gaze. "Pretty high," he said. "What kind of eyes did you say the man had? Blue?"

"No, green. Bright green, like emerald," I answered confidently, and for one brief moment I thought he would believe I wasn't making things up.

"Daniela, we know that you have exceptionally, even unusually keen eyesight; but even this being the case, I don't think you could have distinguished someone's eye color from this far." He patted me affectionately on the back. "Your story was very well put together. However, you must admit that it's just a story. Or you must have dreamed it all." He forced a smile and not knowing what else to say, asked, "Care for a snowball fight?"

"Not really. I'd like to stay outside and...uh... build a snowman". I could hardly find my words. I felt tears welling up and hiding just beneath the surface, tears that I did not want Father to see. I turned on my heels and walked away.

I was finally by myself, with my hurt feelings and unanswered questions as my only companions. My father didn't tell me fair and square that I was a liar. I thought it was nice of him to let me save face. But why did I have to save face? Why wouldn't he believe me? Why...? Ugh, all those whys!

I kept walking among the trees with snow-laden branches recalling the events of that day which I wished I could just erase and start all over. I recalled waking up that morning and rushing to greet the sunrise. Jack Frost had made ice flowers bloom on glass; I had to open the window to see outside. I took in the cold air of the first day of December, thinking happy thoughts about winter break drawing near. I was just about to close the window and get dressed for school, when I saw him standing right there between the plum tree and the apricot tree: an unusually tall man with rather long, silvery hair coming out from under the hood covering his head. I froze in amazement.

My mind worked fervently in search of a satisfactory answer to the first and most urgent question that came to my mind: "Who is this?" Part of me wanted to jump back and shut the window, perhaps in a mix of fear and apprehension. The other part was completely mesmerized by the stranger shrouded in a long white cloak.

Leaning into a staff almost as tall as himself, he looked up at me and smiled. There was joy, warmth, and kindness radiating from the emerald green gaze. He seemed quite far, yet somehow his face stood out, appearing oddly close and clear in every detail. I felt my heart singing, happiness flowing through me, and my hand rose almost by itself. I waved to the stranger who waved back to me. "It can only be Santa Claus," my mind bellowed. "Winter is here, and who knows, maybe he's just gotten around earlier this year". So, Santa is not just a story! I pulled away from the window, ran out of my room and down the stairs, shouting with excitement.

"I've just seen Santa! He's out there in our backyard!"

My parents and Grandma turned at once. "What are you up to?" my dad said tilting his head sideways, looking mildly amused.

My mom pointed at my pajamas, visibly irritated. "You won't have time to eat a decent breakfast," she said. That was typical: my dietary intake and school report were her top concern outweighing everything else. I paused for a moment, and looked at my family in dismay. You gotta be kidding! I just saw Santa Claus standing in our backyard, and the only thing that registered with my mom was me wearing pajamas? I surely didn't get my parents.

As I left home to go to school, just before getting in the car, Grandma looked me in the eyes and said: "Don't tell anybody about what you've seen." I was silent all the way to school, wondering about Grandma's words.

"I hope you are not going to tell this story to anybody," Father echoed Grandma upon dropping me off. I had no intention to follow the advice of either. What are friends for if not for sharing exciting things?

Of course, I had done everything that my father and grandmother had explicitly told me not to do, and as a result I infuriated Comrade Caran, got myself in time out, became, one more time, the subject of ridicule among my classmates, and in the end there I was pacing the backyard, feeling sad and alone in the aftermath of a pretty terrible day. I wandered aimlessly through the white and silent landscape. What if I had listened to Grandma, and just shut up? That didn't feel right either. I thought all over again about the attempts that I made to re-tell my parents what had happened that morning, how much I hoped to find a better audience among the kids at school, and how bad I felt because everything went just the opposite of what I expected. I sighed, very much aware of the heaviness in my heart.

I walked out of our backyard and into the bordering thickets. The gray and heavy sky hanging low above my head was signaling that a lot more snow was on the way. The wind, very mild until then, turned into a breeze as thin and sharp as a razor blade. I didn't care, though, about going back, since there was no one at home with whom I could share my concerns. Whenever I found myself in the patch of woods behind our house, I spoke out loud. I trusted that the fairies listened. So, I raised my voice a little to cover the whistling winds.

"None of my friends care about those things I care about. And among the adults who do, those are just slippery like eels: they dance around my questions, at best throwing at me crumbs that are not enough to satisfy my hunger, but only make it worse. I want..."

I stopped and stomped my feet. There was a powerful desire, a prayer and a longing resounding within. But also, at that moment, it occurred to me that if I were to get any answers, I had to keep pushing for them. Nothing would just fall on my lap simply because I wanted it. It dawned on me that I had been holding on to fears which I had never admitted to have, the fear of the very answers I had been seeking. That whole thought process was strange. I felt silly, and a bit of a coward too. Precisely because of those fears, I had never been able to get Grandma to answer any of my questions. I never pushed far enough nor fought for answers, afraid of what I might hear, and scared about a certain inconvenient truth that could have been brought up in conversation. Inconvenient truth: yes, there was such a thing, and the simple thought of it arising in a discussion with Grandma made me feel sick to my stomach. Some things are best left alone, and I knew that Grandmother wouldn't let me get away with it, if somehow the incident I had in mind would ever surface again in conversation. It was one of the reasons that made me prefer the pain of uncertainty to the risk of hearing disappointing answers about who I am and who I belong with. The train of thoughts halted abruptly, and in anger, I launched a mighty kick against a tree trunk. I bounced back, and landed on my butt while the tree shook off its load of snow dumping it all on my head. I heard a chuckle.

"Now, you didn't make a snowman: you almost turned yourself into one." Grandma caught up with me. She helped me shake the snow off my clothes. Meanwhile, my mind kept spinning threads and strategizing about weaving them into a conversation with her. The fear of being denied answers or hearing inconvenient truths still held on to me. I had just made peace with being different in some ways in comparison to other children. Still, how much different was I? As usual, each time that thought came, I began reasoning against it with equal strength. I couldn't be that "special". I didn't want to be rare: I wanted to be myself. I wanted to find my place, and I somehow knew that my place, whatever that was, involved me being more like Grandma. Ok then; maybe I was a little different. Maybe not everyone can talk to plants, animals, sense the presence of fairies and fairy-like beings, and see colors. But among those who do – because, come on, at least part of the children my age could do the same, right? – why were they hiding instead of sharing freely, the way I had tried to do? I also did not understand why most adults were so intolerant, even resentful, and adamantly pounded their fists against tables while insisting that "extraordinary" things only belonged in fairy tales for little kids or were nothing but legends? Why couldn't the majority of adults get along with the fact that the fairy phenomena recorded from long ago are still ongoing nowadays? Assuming that some, if not most children were born with what my aunt calls "gifts", what happens to these children when growing older? Was the magical nature that maybe kids naturally have, fading away by itself? Did some people choose to preserve their gifts and become like my own grandmother, or like my aunt? Was there anything else that I should know about people's magic abilities, because assuming that I had any, I didn't want to lose them, no matter the cost.

I took a deep breath and looked at Grandma. Our eyes met. Grandma and I shared a connection and a sense of kinship that, as I perceived it, reached beyond family ties. Her eyes would light up in a mix of pride and affection when telling her daughters and their close friends "how much I took after her." I didn't understand exactly what she meant by that. I couldn't make warts or nasty skin growths go away with rainwater, herbs, and weird words muttered under breath. Nor did I know how to talk to clouds, sprinkle water in circles, and make rain come about. Yet Grandma could do all these, and a whole lot more. I always believed that if we were alike as she said we were, then maybe she would teach me all what she knew.

I caught her gaze again, and I seized the opportunity. I wanted Grandma to help me shed light over the questions that I had. I wanted her to teach me everything she knew, convinced that I would be able to learn it all, fast. I was carefully choosing my words, dwindling between self-doubt and hope.

"What is it, my dear," Grandma asked, given my unusually long silence.

"Granny, what kind of a witch are you?" With a will of their own, the words flew off my lips. In fact, I shouted out as loud as I could to make sure that she'd hear me over the strong gusts of wind. I realized my mistake, but it was too late. She stopped furiously yanking me by the arm. I tripped and fell. A volcano stood about to erupt in my chest. I had spoiled everything.

"Have you lost your mind? Do you want us all in jail?" Her voice was rasp, heavy, and threatening. This Grandma I had hardly ever seen. Yet her words brought me back to a very harsh reality. There was prohibition and, in some cases, even persecution against almost everything pertaining to the spiritual. Any involvement with the occult was, at least in theory, punishable by law. "We live in glorious Communist times..." Comrade Caran's voice resounded in my ears.

"I won't tell anybody," I said promptly, which didn't appease Grandma.

"How can I trust you? I warned you to keep silent about the man you saw this morning, but you didn't listen. Do you realize what kind of a situation you have created for yourself and for your parents? "

I understood her point and felt guilty. I didn't want to hurt my family, of course, but I felt compelled to share anyway. I needed to find those like myself, and where to look if not among my peers? I could not come to terms with the fact that other kids were complete strangers to experiences such as my own. I told Grandma all my thoughts in just one breath, and fell silent.

The wind died down suddenly, and snowflakes began to make their way toward the ground. Their sight separated me ever so briefly from my worries. We walked back silently, holding hands.

Chapter 2

I pushed away the arithmetic notebook and leaned forward to prop up my chin on the desk. With my mind gone haywire, I couldn't concentrate on homework. I wanted to have a discussion with Grandma. Reluctant as she seemed, I could sense that she would still want to answer at least some of my questions. I didn't want to give up. How much worse could things get? Mom had informed me that my teacher required a psychological evaluation. She wanted a specialist's explanation for what she called borderline sane behavior. Her request infuriated my parents, but they had to comply.

With a flicker and a buzz, the light in the house went out. I stared into the night outside. The shapes of the trees were barely distinguishable. Occasional gusts of wind smashed snowflakes as large as butterflies against the window. The water inside radiators crackled: a disjointed and funny-sounding song against a backdrop of absolute silence. I watched my thoughts flowing slow and clear like a large river: what do fairies do on a winter night such as this? Was the man I saw that morning also a fairy? What about…

My mother walking in suddenly made me jump. The thick carpet in the corridor muffled her steps so her entering my room caught me entirely by surprise.

"Don't you feel…" (I could tell she was choosing her words carefully) "lonely, sitting in the dark like this? I brought you a candle. Here, take this." Mother put the old, massive silver candle holder on my desk. "Don't drip wax on the rugs when you come downstairs for dinner, dear". She patted me on the head and I drew closer. "You are such a smart girl," she said. "I don't understand why you are so persistent with these stories of yours. You'd make a great writer though," she added with a smile. "Your fairies would fit so well in a book." Then, Mother turned serious again, held me in front of her and said: "At least for now, you must stop talking about fairies as if they were real."

"But they are real," I insisted. "They are real to me. And you know, not all of them are fairies. There are also other kinds of beings, and colors that sometimes surround people and objects..."

Mom didn't let me finish. She spoke about the upcoming appointment with the psychologist, and about the dangerous situation I could create for all of us if anybody from the outside suspected our family being involved with anything pertaining to the occult. I said nothing. Mom invited me to come downstairs with her if I was uncomfortable sitting all by myself in semidarkness. I wondered who was actually more uncomfortable with the dark... and a thought flashed through my mind.

"Is Grandma downstairs, too," I asked. Mom shook her head and told me that Grandma retired early, asking Vica, our impromptu housemaid, to bring her tea and a light snack in her room. This was unusual. Then, sensing what I was looking for, Mother added: "And I would like you not to pester Grandma with any silly questions about magic. Understood?"

I was not hungry at all, but bringing that up would have caused even more trouble. My mom was obsessed with me being too thin and too frail – which I didn't think I was. Anyway, I didn't want any more of her attention that night since I needed to be invisible to her for my plan to work. I thought that for strategic purposes, I must therefore have dinner, hungry or not.

I sat at the table. Everyone seemed quite relaxed, which surprised me. I was very glad that none of the day's events made it into conversation. I finished quickly and took my plates to the sink, adding them to the pile that Vica would wash at some point.

"Good night" I said, trying to sound tired. I headed upstairs and pretended to go to my room. I did actually open and close the door loudly, but didn't walk inside. Instead, I tiptoed toward the end of the corridor. I passed Vica's room and my parents' bedroom, and I found myself in front of Grandma's door. I paused and listened for any noise coming from downstairs. I had left my parents sitting by a roaring fire steeped in conversation over cups of molten wine. I knew for sure that they wouldn't come upstairs anytime soon. Vica had not even begun to clean off the table when I left the dining room, and I knew she'd be busy for quite a while. I had plenty of time.

I got my ear closer to the door. The coldness of the massive, polished-to-glow wood sent shivers down my spine as it touched my cheek. I heard Grandma talking in a soft voice. It seemed like a dialogue, but I could only hear one of the speakers. No matter how much I strained my ears and even held my breath, I couldn't hear to whom she was talking. Nor could I understand everything that she said. There were words, some of them names, that I haven't heard nor read anywhere else. She stopped suddenly.

"Come in, Daniela." I was stunned. I did not move, and had been barely breathing not to betray my presence. Yet in the exact same moment I thought about knocking at her door, just before raising my hand, Grandma asked me to come in. How did she know I was there? Among four other people in the house, how did she pick up that it was me and not someone else?

"How did you know it was me? And to whom were you talking to," I asked – my voice probably betraying surprise – while I closed the door carefully.

"I was just singing to myself while knitting. Would you like to read something together? Tea? There's still hot water in the kettle. And milk, right there, in the small pitcher. You can pour a cup for me, also…"

Clearly, Grandma was trying to distract me from the questions I just asked upon entering the room. The gas lantern and the candles on the table gave a soft, golden light that made the room look even friendlier than usual, if such a thing was even possible. I noticed that the yarn, needles, and whatever Grandma was knitting, was tucked away neatly in a basket sitting on the floor. It was obvious even for me, a nine years old kid, that she was not knitting while I was listening at the door. I suddenly caught a light scent of flowers floating through the air. Fresh flowers? I asked myself while my eyes stumbled upon the only flower vase in the room sitting empty on top of the drawer-chest.

"Where did the woman go, Grandma," I heard myself asking, yet having no idea where those words came from. I felt embarrassed for what I just said, but somehow, I knew with certainty that a woman had been in the room.

"Do you see anybody in here, sweetie," Grandma asked, her green eyes fixated on my face. I looked around, and shook my head.

"Look again carefully," she said. I squinted, strained my eyes, creased my brow till it hurt, and saw... nothing. The scent of flowers lingered for a short while, wafting right by my nose, then it disappeared. The candle under the wooden icon in the corner of the room flickered as if a breeze had moved it despite the fact that I felt no air draft.

"Well, maybe there isn't anybody in the room," Grandma said, and I thought she sounded a little disappointed. I had been suspecting that Grandma could talk to fairies, but I wasn't certain though. However, I knew that she talked to the spirits of the departed ones. There had been times when I felt I could do the same. After all, Grandma and I were alike... but then, why didn't I see anybody in the room?

We both fell silent. In the candlelight, Grandma's eyes shimmered like green pools of water.

"Grandma, I'm so sorry for...everything." I didn't know what else to say.

She sighed, then continued.

"You made a mess bigger than yourself. Now you would like to mend things, don't you? Only, my dear, it's a bit too late. Your parents are very upset with me for allowing you to get so close to our practices, lore and folklore as some call them, ahem! I learned from my grandmother, who learned from her grandmother, and so on, and I hoped that one day I'd pass all the knowledge on to you. But I've been totally wrong. It's too dangerous. We cannot trust you to keep it a secret to begin with." There was both resignation and sternness in her voice.

My cheeks went burning, and in the blink of an eye I shifted from sad to furious. Before Grandma could say anything else, I poured out all my frustration.

"You, Aunt Camellia, and even Mother allowed me close enough to see a lot, yet none of you nor your friends had ever explained anything clearly to me. I've been watching you, and I've been meddling into your affairs ever since I can remember. Even as a toddler, I crawled into your circles and messed up with your spell ingredients whenever I thought no one was watching. So, I do have some understanding of these old ways, as you call them, but for the most part, I don't. I don't fully comprehend my own experiences, nor do I know what to do about the things I see and hear. I'm not just a strange, deranged child, as my teacher calls me, am I? None of my friends believed me when I told them how pretty our cat was, her fur glowing green and bright blue. Don't they have cats of their own, glowing with nice colors? Why is nobody talking about it? Why does nobody want to talk about the fairies in their gardens, the spirits of their homes, the voices in the trees…Is everyone else better than I am at keeping it all secret?"

Grandma came to sit on the bed's edge next to me. She held me close and kissed me on the forehead.

"Oy, what would you have done, first thing upon being told that you do possess a gift, and you are indeed special, and therefore a strange child? Let me tell you what: you'd run out straight to your so-called friends and brag about your gifts, creating more turmoil and bringing trouble upon us. I have been impatient to teach you. Yes, I allowed you to meddle into our affairs, that's part of your apprenticeship. This is how your great-grandmother started teaching me. You have to see it first, live it, and find out for yourself whether you belong or not. And you did. Oh, you did so well, without yourself even knowing how well you had been doing. You picked up more things that we all thought you could. However, you began to demand answers. I let you feel your way through, telling you as little as possible given your big mouth. We also had to slow your impatience down a bit, and at times divert your attention because…you see…these are very different times then the ones of my own childhood. But you are too young, irresponsible, and yes, the times we live are so different and difficult…" Grandma hesitated.

"Because of the Communist regime?" I jumped in, completing the sentence. I must have spoken pretty loudly because she shushed me, and then nodded silently. I made a desperate plea.

"But Grandma, I belong with you and these old ways, witchery, or whatever you call them. I will keep my mouth shut, I promise. I'll do everything you ask from me. I'll do great, and make you and Great-Grandmother proud!"

"Witchcraft, not witchery. But how did the word come to you? We call ourselves medicine women, doftoroaie, or spiritual healers, not witches, at least not overtly. We don't seek to put ourselves in direct enmity with the Church, which is the only form of spirituality tolerated by the actual regime, as you already know. Tolerated, beware; not embraced, let alone welcomed."

"But this regime will eventually come to an end, right? Aunt Camellia divined and saw it coming, so…"

"SHUSH!! Have you lost your mind? Never mention, even dare to think such thoughts. Many people have paid with their lives for having entertained such beliefs."

"I know, but I can keep a secret, really. I only need to know that it is a secret, and I won't let it out…I haven't told anybody about my aunt's divination skills, nor about Mother's – yeah, I know that Mom wants to be "modern" and pretends not to care about witchy stuff – I haven't said a word about you, Miss Constance, and Miss Ileana, never mentioned your charms and healings, and never spoke about all the people who come to you secretly, for help. But I truly believed that all children can see fairies, or colors at least, and I could never understand why we can't have a conversation about it: it's not the same thing as doing magic, is it?"

"Yes, I mean no.... It isn't, yet it is the same darn thing. Oh, forget it! None of this is typical, or accepted by this "modern" society we live in. The government considers mystic and occult practices unhealthy for individuals and dangerous to social order. And you are short tempered, big-mouthed, careless, fearless in a pretty stupid way, and as it seems to me, unaware of what could happen..."

"No, I'm not!!" I nearly shouted, evidently in denial of what was only a brief list of my shortcomings and oblivious to the fact that indeed I could have become a danger to myself and others.

"Keep quiet, and don't you dare to raise your voice in my presence!" Grandma stood up suddenly tall and proud. I did the same. "Sit," she said curtly as one would command a dog. Her voice sounded almost threatening, same as it did sound earlier in the garden. My knees obeyed immediately, getting me seated on the spot; it happened before my brain had even processed her words to make an informed decision.

"Yes, you are! You are also conveniently forgetful. Do you remember what happened when you cursed Marius? Do you remember what I cautioned you against?"

Of course, I did remember; I only hoped that Grandmother would not. My fear that she'd bring up that very inconvenient truth came to pass. The episode flashed through my mind. My hands went icy-cold and my palms sweaty.

Chapter 3

The episode Grandma mentioned felt strangely remote although it had occurred less than six months ago. Back then, Marius and I were still sworn enemies. We were neighbors, and I was very grateful for the eight feet tall fence surrounding his family's property. However, our paths crossed quite often since our homes were part of a small cluster where everybody knew everybody. Marius was almost two years older and loved being the boss. I loved being my own boss, and would not take any orders from him. Marius was pesky. I was short-tempered. We were both good at holding grudges for trivial reasons and bent on revenge, even for petty things. Marius' determination to bully me and my own refusal to lay low set up the tone for our interaction since we first met.

The day that my grandmother asked me to remember was the first one for me returning to play outdoors. I had just overcome a serious illness that kept me bedridden for a month, and in a wheelchair for almost four. On the day in question, I finally made my reappearance on our alley walking instead of wheeling myself around. As I neared the playground, I saw some kids, Marius among them. I expected my slow and awkward walk to become the new target of his ridicule. I wasn't sure I wanted to confront him, but I didn't want to turn around and act cowardly either.

"Hi, Walky-Ducky," he said as soon as he saw me.

I told him where to go and what to do with himself. Seeing his aggravation was simply delightful. Marius gave me a dirty look, leaped closer, and grabbed me by the shoulder threatening life and limb. I swung my arm as far back as his grip allowed, and then punched him in the stomach with gusto. Marius let go instantly curling in pain. We had fist-fought several times before. He was bigger but also slower, intimidating other kids only because of his size and attitude. I was rather small, thin, but very fast and agile; or, better said, I used to be that way. I ignored how heavy and cumbersome my lower body had become due to the prolonged illness. I had engaged Marius without thinking that I'd be unable to move quick enough. Wheeling myself around the house had strengthened my arms, but my legs were no match. Avoiding my next punch, Marius pushed me from the side. I lost balance and fell down. The kick I received in the ribs left me breathless for a few moments.

Marius kept calling me names, while walking backwards, still holding on to his belly. I got up and picked up a rock. I threw it while Marius was mounting his bike, but missed him narrowly. He turned around and rode towards me. Kids screamed in horror. I bent over for another rock, but Marius already got near my side, leaned towards, and pushed me forcefully. I lost balance again and landed in a flowerbed. I stood up on my knees, watching him ride away. I yelled from the top of my lungs: "I'm cursing you! I wish you dead, Marius!"

I got up, and walked into our front yard. I didn't even know how the idea of casting a curse came to me, but I surely meant it. I didn't know how to actually do it, but I held such hate and anger! I thought that if I could only send those feelings Marius' way, it would have been enough to harm him.

I kneeled on the freshly aerated garden soil. My fingers sunk in the dirt and started to dig mechanically. My eyes fell on a chip of wood still hanging on my clothes since I fell down. I picked it up. The sight and feeling of the splinter in my hand boosted my anger which became outright hate. I felt my blood boiling.

"Your bones will break ", I said, thinking of Marius, and cracked the wooden chip between my fingers. I dumped the pieces in the hole I had dug, covered them up with dirt, and then I slammed a rock on top, imagining it as a tombstone. I said out loud "Now you're dead, and I'm done with you once and for all!"

Half way toward the backdoor, I bumped into Grandma. She looked at me with concern.

"What happened? What have you been up to?"

I told her the whole story. Grandma frowned while listening. When I finished, her eyes looked like the sky before a storm: dark, and threatening. She raised her hand and I braced myself in anticipation of the heavy slap. Her hand landed firmly on my shoulder, instead.

"What if Marius didn't even mean anything offensive by calling you Walky-Ducky? I know that you don't get along at all, but do you realize that about half the times you end up fighting, it is because of you provoking him? You expect him to be mean; you strike out first because you anticipate him to act meanly, and then you get upset when he strikes back. He's not an angel, but honestly, I've been wondering who's actually worse among the two of you. As far as the curse concerns, we must have a conversation right now."

We walked inside the house. Grandma just finished making coffee. As my anger cooled off little by little, I felt uncertain about the righteousness of everything I'd said and done that afternoon. What if I wouldn't have snapped at Marius when he first called me Walky-Ducky? What if I had just ignored him? What if Grandma was right in stating that most likely, he just made a joke, a tasteless one but still a joke. At first, I didn't want to admit that I could be wrong, but as Grandma continued to talk, I started to get a different impression of the role that I played in what had just happened. Who knows how many conflicts I could have avoided? I felt guilt nudging me, but I wasn't ready to fully admit that I was in the wrong. Then I thought again of the impromptu curse, and I felt ashamed. How was I going to live with myself if something bad really happened to Marius? The more I thought of it, the worse I felt. I would have rather preferred him calling me names, fist fighting, playing tricks, even tasteless ones, over knowing he was hurt or dead and weighing on my consciousness.

"Grandma", I said, "can I stop the curse, or take it back somehow? Do you really think it is going to hurt Marius?"

Grandma let out a heavy sigh.

"Oy, what did you get yourself into? Who taught you to cast a curse in the first place? It can ruin your life…"

"As it ruined Aunt Camellia's?" My question popped, betraying my excitement about the subject. My aunt was quite a character, and her life's story, filled with messy intrigues and destructive magic, was something that I came to know in detail as a result of many hours of eavesdropping.

"Don't you dare!" Grandma pointed her index toward me, and I almost felt the short poking in my belly, although her finger didn't actually touch me. She lowered her hand, waved briskly, then asked again, sighing:

"Who taught you how to cast a curse?"

"Nobody. It just came to me. I don't know where it came from, but it felt familiar, like I've done it before, although I know for certain that I haven't."

"Did it feel like someone else was guiding you, like speaking to your mind, or …moving your hands?" I noticed the hesitation in her voice, although I didn't know what it meant.

"Absolutely not. It came from me alone, and from my anger. But yes, it felt oddly familiar, and while it felt right when I did it, it feels less so now."

Grandma seemed a little relieved, and again I didn't understand why.

"What about Aunt Camellia?" I asked. "She's the only one among us whom I ever heard talking about casting curses and wishing all sorts of nasty things to different people. She looks unhappy for the most part, and angry… She tells me that all people are mean, so I should learn to defend myself, don't make friends, and never trust anybody."

"Leave her alone, and don't listen to her. She needs to mind her own business. I'll have a word with your aunt."

"What about the curse I cast? Can you help me undo it, please?"

"You can only pray, and wish for a chance to tell Marius that you are sorry about the misunderstanding. Don't ever mention the curse. We can do a little ritual tonight so that..."

The phone rang. Grandma went down the hallway to answer. When she returned to the kitchen her face was whiter than a sheet of paper. I had a nasty feeling.

"Marius got hit by a car while riding his bike about thirty minutes ago. He was just taken to the hospital. His grandmother called and asked me to go over to their house."

Grandma stormed toward the door but stopped abruptly and turned toward me:

"This answer's the question I guess; in case you are still wondering whether you cast your curse well. Oy, this is one of the saddest days in my life." Grandma spun on her heels and left.

As soon as the door closed behind Grandma, I dragged myself to my room and sunk into preparing a little ritual of my own fashioning which I believed would help Marius. I prayed, and asked those fairies goodly inclined toward me for guidance about how to repair the harm I had caused. I didn't know specifically who those fairies would be, but I had a keen sense that there were some among them willing to pitch in. I said that I would wholeheartedly agree to pay any price for the undoing of the curse and its consequences, and hoped that they'd take my offer[2]. I was uncertain about what was worse: having hurt Marius, or having disappointed Grandma.

The memory had engulfed me completely with its vividness. I had not left Grandma's room, of course, yet I felt as if I went away on a long trip and barely came back. The candles, the furniture, the old clock seemed strange to look at, as if I hadn't seen them in a long time. At least something became clear: I knew who I was. I was not a deranged kid as my teacher suggested, but someone who inherited the knack for magic as it had been transmitted through generations before me. But would Grandma ever be willing to teach me all that she knew? I had the gift, but not the knowledge on how to use it, and without the former, the first didn't hold much value – or so I thought.

Then Grandma spoke:

"Now, did you keep the promises you made back then?"

"I guess I did. I didn't cast any curses. Aside from little protection charms, I didn't cast any big spells either, but that's simply because I don't know how, and nobody wants to teach me." I landed heavily on the last part of the sentence hoping to get my point across. But grandma ignored my attempt and continued talking with mocked resignation:

"No, you didn't really keep your promise, at least not for the part that concerns us the most. First, you still give in to anger very easily although I'm glad that you haven't cursed anyone over the past months. Second, you hardly ever follow any advice. You have a mind of your own and disregard all cautioning. Being brave and creative are wonderful qualities, but you do expose yourself by showing off foolishly and by giving in to anger much too easily which is neither brave nor smart."

Albeit grudgingly, I had to admit that Grandma's point was valid.

"Granny, for how long have there been witches... I mean medicine women in our family?"

"Since forever," she said, smiling tiredly. "The earliest historical record of our family goes back to the fifteenth century, and so do the earliest stories of your great-great-grandmothers doing this kind of spirit work. Their ways mingled Christian teachings with ancient knowledge that had been around since the dawn of time. I believe that even when it skipped a generation or two, being a medicine woman or man, or a psychic, has always been a thing in our family. But here we are, some five hundred years later…" Grandmother sighed, leaving the sentence unfinished. She didn't even bother to hide her disappointment.

"Why is Aunt Camellia so…different?" I asked, choosing my words carefully.

"Your aunt has chosen to meet life with anger and resentment. She had a successful yet short acting career that ended when she ran away with a man. They married, although I did not give my consent. Camellia has a mind of her own, very much like you do. Their unhappy marriage fell apart a few years later. She's been carrying the anger and disappointment of an outcome that she is entirely responsible for, although she would not admit to anything. The fault is never hers, but someone else's, so as the victim that she believes she is, Camelia feels entitled to hate everyone else."

"She does cast curses, doesn't she? And I heard she's very good at it. But why can't she do good spells, I mean do nice things for others and for herself to be happy, healthy, or to attract a husband which I know she wishes for?"

It took Grandma a while to answer. I thought she was revisiting unhappy memories, things that she would have rather not brought to the surface. She poured tea absentmindedly, apparently not even realizing that the water had gone cold. The room was getting colder too.

"To cast a real curse, a curse that works, you need a lot of hate and anger as you found out by yourself, unfortunately. The more anger and hate one harbors, the easier it becomes to cast curses. It also becomes an easy outlet for all that energy, and for some of our kind it becomes a very natural one, too. The more curses one does cast, the more comfortable he or she becomes with releasing anger that way. The more anger and resentment one builds within themselves, the greater the need to unburden becomes. Unfortunately, whenever in a tight spot, casting curses and binding spells is what people like Camellia will pull out, like circus magicians pulling rabbits out of a hat. In short, this is how someone's entire life gets poisoned with hate and anger, two very strong energies fueling up an ability turned harmful. In the end, the ability turns against those who misuse it. From the outside, it seems that the entire outpouring of hate and anger concentrated within a curse only affects the targeted recipient. Yet, the curses your aunt cast right and left against her rivals, destroyed her life more than they had ever destroyed anyone else's. People have recovered from the harm she has caused to them; but she has never recovered from the anger and hate she has been entertaining for all these years."

"I will learn not to give in to anger, nor hate. I'll work on it. If you could only train me into, you know..." I left the sentence unfinished, and let my imploring gaze speak for me. Each ounce of my tiny being was longing to do magic, live magic, and breath magic like Grandma and Great-Grandma, and like all those amazing women before them.

Grandma stood up, and started to pace the room. Strangely, I could almost hear her thoughts. Deep down inside her heart a battle was taking place. Could she give herself permission to defy my parents' dispositions regarding me? Could she find ways to pass on to me what was nearest and dearest to her, the legacy of a long line of magic – practicing women? Would that really serve my best interest? Should she follow along with what my parents asked from her and banish me for good from her circles? I had probably forgotten to breathe while waiting for the verdict, when Grandma spoke again:

"You, my dear, you need to keep up with the modern world you live in – this is probably best for you, and for all of us. Forget about learning anything of the old ways. At least for now."

Chapter 4

Heartbroken, I left Grandma and walked to my room through the dark corridor. At first, I felt anger and a tremendous desire to do something bad, to hurt someone in revenge for my own unhappiness. Things MUST line up, as I want them to, or else! If I hurt, people around me should hurt too! The thoughts caught me by surprise. No, it wasn't the first time I felt that way, but I at that moment, like never before, I was aware of both the thought and its inappropriateness which I believed was an improvement already. That was Aunt Camellia's type of thinking, I told myself. And then it dawned on me: I had inherited my Grandmother's talent and a good deal of Aunt Camellia's temperament added to my own innate affinity for trouble. In other words, my little person was something akin to a keg of gunpowder. If I were to acquire Grandma's skills – assuming she'd teach me – I would then possess not only a perfect script for disaster, but also a whole arsenal to make it happen. Of course, Grandma could not take any more risks with me. This was what she wanted me to understand. I admitted to myself that I did fall short on my promise indeed. I had not cast any more curses, but I haven't done anything beyond that. I haven't done anything to become less belligerent and less vindictive. I sometimes felt remorse for hurting Marius or the occasional victims of the fights that I'd pick. But such episodes of remorse were usually short-lived: I didn't want to appear as weak and soft. Upon hearing of Marius' misfortune, I had wanted to run and beg for a pardon right away. Yet a week later I was still making up excuses to not go visit him at the hospital. Almost five months later, I still had not had a conversation with him and I wasn't even sure why.

Although sad beyond measure, I kept hanging on desperately to those last words that Grandma uttered before I left her room: "At least for now." I had always been an incurable optimist. By the time I reached my own room, I had convinced myself that Grandma only meant that I had to prove myself worthy before she could teach me anything. I kept telling myself that hers' wasn't a definitive refusal, and it wasn't supposed to last for too long either. If I had only known how to send a charm, or cast a spell to fog everyone's memory of that morning and start anew tomorrow!

Tomorrow: the word resounded in my head brassy and dissonant like a badly played bugle. I stood frozen in the middle of my room. Outside of my rapid breath, I could hear the distant humming of snowplows cleaning the roads. Therefore, school will be open tomorrow whether the power will be back or not in our part of the city. I had not done any homework. The perspective of showing up unprepared, and having to explain to Comrade Caran why that happened was plainly terrifying. I looked at the clock on the wall. The phosphorus hands were drawing a perfect vertical across the quadrant. "It's not even tomorrow," I said in panic. "It's today!!"

I walked by the window and looked at the postcard-perfect landscape: a pale moon glimpsing through clouds made the snow sparkle like diamond dust. Engulfed by the beauty of the winter night, I felt my mind suspended, floating, impervious to any thought. Space and time disappeared. I stood there mesmerized, for who knows how long, till the loud roar of an engine coming from our alley yanked me back to reality. The dream-like state was gone, but so was the anxiety I had felt moments ago. I could almost hear all the wheels in my head turning, in search of a solution. I wasn't panicking, although I knew that I was indeed in trouble. And because I wasn't panicking, the solution surfaced shortly: play sick.

That was easier said than done. With my mom being a medical professional, just stating that I don't feel well wouldn't be enough to convince her. On the other hand, she easily worried about my health, so I felt I had a chance. I fell asleep, fervently desiring for some sign of illness to show up. I wished for something to happen, anything that would convince my mom to make me stay home. For once in my life, I would have been totally happy to be commended to bed rest.

A cold touch on my forehead woke me up. I heard my mom muttering angrily something about fever, and me playing in the snow for too long. I didn't open my eyes right away, my brain feeling all fuzzy. I was shivering, and any attempt to move sent shooting pains throughout my body.

"Why is it so cold here? Isn't time for school yet?" I could hear my own voice sounding hoarse, and the words I barely uttered grazed my throat like sandpaper. I was miserable. I had a recollection, vague at first, then getting clearer, of the night before. I remember telling myself that being ill would have been a better alternative to facing my teacher. And there I was, shivering and with a sore throat. Was this the outcome of my own desire, the one that I kindled and took with me in my sleep last night? Did I make a deliberate choice to get ill? It could have been nothing more than a coincidence, or the obvious result of me spending hours in the snow – ignoring the icy cold, soaking wet socks and pants – although I preferred the other version much better. I did feel off the whole evening, although I blamed feeling that way on all the reasons that I had to be sad. Whatever the truth behind my sudden illness, I didn't have to face Comrade Caran nor the pediatric psychologist right away. A bout of cough brought tears to my eyes. Suddenly, A bulb went off in my mind, and I got a glimpse of how to take advantage of the situation. If I could only get a moment alone with Grandma! I felt I had found a way to make her change her mind and teach me all that she knew about magic. All of a sudden, my own sickness didn't bother me that much.

"Here's some hot grits with butter. Your grandmother prepared them for you" Vica adjusted my pillows so I could sit up. Then she carefully placed in front of me the tray with the steaming bowl of grits.

"Where's Grandma," I asked, trying to ignore what felt like a bunch of straw stuffed inside my throat and chest tickling and hurting at the same time. I burst into a cough. When the cough finally stopped, I was too exhausted and too afraid to even try to swallow the tiniest bit of grits. I motioned Vica to take away the tray.

"Just a bit, Daniela, please take just a little bit. These grits are very soft and soaking with butter, just what you need." I closed my eyes, and moved my hand signaling again no. I was getting tired of the whole situation. I hadn't seen Grandmother since the night we last spoke. Or maybe she came only when I was asleep to avoid more questions and pleading. I thought that even if she'd come, I couldn't speak with her without that damn cough choking me each time I'd whisper more than three or four words. Despite all the medicines my mother shoved into me, I wasn't one tiny bit better than the previous day when I woke up with a sore throat and high fever.

Father walked in. My face must have shown clearly how glad I was to see him, because he sat down on the edge of my bed and without any other ado, asked: "So, what story do you want to hear?"

"The Odyssey", I whispered, thrilled over the unexpected treat. I was perfectly able to read and I loved doing so, but still there was no greater delight than listening to Father or Grandma telling stories. Father would actually play the characters and do the voices, too. The dialogues were, of course, changing slightly from one retelling to another, and there were occasional twists and turns in the original plots that initial authors had no idea would ever happen. Over the past year or so, story time with Father became sparse. He traveled more than ever before. Also, he and mom argued more than ever before.

"Hey, are you ready?" Father asked, noticing that my attention had momentarily slipped away. I nodded, and shortly after, I was assailing the city of Troy alongside Achilles' famous warriors, the Myrmidons. I could have listened forever, especially to the part where Odysseus tricks the Trojans to open the gates and usher the gigantic wooden horse into the city. Father knew that the part about the Trojan Horse was a favorite of mine, so he lengthened the tale by adding countless details, things that he had either studied or just made up for my entertainment. That afternoon in particular, the story spoke to me in ways that it never did before. The conquest of Troy took on a whole different meaning. I had to be smart like Odysseus, if I was to get behind the walls that Grandma surrounded herself with.

The story ended, and I wished Father and I could sit and talk like we had not done in a long time. Carefully not to trigger another bout of coughing, I whispered: "I wish I were Odysseus."

"You can't be him. You're Daniela. But you can be as smart as Odysseus, and equally brave."

"But can I have a bow like his?' My other favorite part in 'The Odyssey' was that where Ulysses shows his prowess with his bow and overcomes his enemies almost single-handed.

"As soon as you get well, we're making a new bow. You have outgrown the old one anyway. And there'll be a surprise for you also."

"A surprise? What is it? A new quiver and arrows?" The cough cut me short. Father handed me the bottle of cough-syrup, the sight of which made me want to throw up for how much of it I already had.

"Grandma will be with you soon," Father added. "I drove her to pick up Ms. Constantza. They'll be with you within moments to take care of your cough. I don't understand how these things work, but since all medicine has failed, I'm open to let them try their thing. I thought you would actually like it since it's witchy just to your taste."

My eyes widened. Father allowing Grandma and her friend to heal me? That was unheard of and unimagined. Father was the most pragmatic person I knew. For me, myths and old stories were carriers of hidden, occult knowledge surviving from a distant past; for Father, myths and stories were nothing but literature meant to entertain and educate. His belief, that magic only had its place in stories, brought us oftentimes at odds with each other. However, he did encourage me to discover the world through exploration, trial and error, and believed that the strong-willed warrior side of me should be encouraged, not suppressed. As far as my magical inclinations, those should be redirected carefully since he truly believed they were just a phase.

Suddenly I heard the argument breaking in the hallway.

"You promised her a new bow? You are telling me that you want to surprise her with archery lessons? Did I hear you correctly? She's a girl, and needs girls' things like pretty dresses and dolls, not weapons."

My stomach churned. I wanted to vomit: I thoroughly disliked dolls, and I absolutely hated to be coerced into the stereotypical girl my mother and aunt had decided I must be "mainstreamed" into. I absolutely didn't mind pretty clothes and jewelry, but I also liked archery and swords, and never shied away from a good fistfight. As for my witchiness, and my obsession with magic in general and fairies in particular, I believed that was my very nature, not even a choice or a preference. I didn't just like it, as I would like some game that I'd get bored with at some point; that was me. I got angrier as Mother continued to talk.

"We need to weed out all these weird things from her mind, boyish stuff and magic in the first place. But you steer her in the wrong direction. Why? You are away for most of the time, and I am left to deal with her."

"Stop it!" Father's voice thundered as he most likely forgot that I could hear their argument. "Two years from now she may be interested in fine arts, or fashion design, or something else, and forget about archery. And even if she won't change her preferences, why do you torture her to fit the mold that you and your sister have determined is the golden standard for femininity? As far as the child's interest in magic, I will reason with her. I believe we have a better chance to convince her with logical arguments rather than suppressing and taking away all things that she loves. "

"Who's taking anything away from her? I want her to be a good girl and not embarrass us with her boyish style – so inappropriate, so not lady-like. And I definitely want her to stay away from the witchy things. I could hardly bring myself to let the old ladies try to cure her, but since nothing else worked so far..."

The voices faded as my parents moved farther away. So, Father intended to get me archery lessons. That was probably the surprise that he had planned.

"Only, if he's not around, Mother will make sure those lessons don't happen," I told myself, and watched the happiness of getting archery lessons and the unhappiness of Mother, allowing them to fight against each other in my mind.

Grandma and her lifelong friend, Ms. Constanza, walked in. The two women carried trays, their contents hidden from sight under white linen towels. I eyed the trays curiously and was mildly suspicious. I believed Father would have had nothing against teas, tinctures, and poultices, but I didn't think he would be happy with anything really witchy being done around me. I was glad he wasn't present. As far as Mother was concerned, in that specific instance she'd get on board with anything that would help me heal. For me, that was the opportunity to convince Grandma to train me as a witch, a doftoroaie, like herself.

"Here, here, little darling," Ms. Constanza spoke, her voice almost a sing-song, and her blue gaze oozing kindness. I had not seen her in a while, so I stretched my arms out for a hug. For a while, my face disappeared squashed against her chest, my spine glad to receive the warmth of her palms. "You'll be well in no time, you'll see," Ms. Constanza continued to speak in the same soft voice that could lull into sleep even the worst among worries.

In the meantime, Grandma had removed the towels covering the trays. She picked an empty cup, and Ms. Constanza took a small pitcher from which she poured water into the cup. She placed the pitcher back onto the tray. Grandma advanced holding the cup. Ms. Constanza placed her hands over Grandma's. They both closed their eyes and murmured something that I could not understand. I had probably forgotten to breathe, and too worried that I'd miss some detail, I probably wasn't blinking either. Then Ms. Constantza picked up a matchbox, struck a match and held the flame over the water cup. Both women whispered something that to my despair I could, again, not understand. Ms. Constanza doused the match into the cup, then threw it into an ashtray prepared in advance for that purpose. A second match sparked its bright flame briefly hovering over the cup before being doused. My hearing, stretched to the limit, had picked up a few words

"As the water douses the flame..." There was the third match coming out of the box. I knew what would follow, so instead of looking at the match and the cup again, I focused on Grandma's lips. "...the charm douses the cough." I smiled victoriously, but only for one moment: I missed the very last sentence they said. Anyway, I made a quick mental note "As the water douses the flame, so the charm douses the cough," and whatever I was supposed to say after this. Four more times flames burned briskly and died with a hiss as they embodied the demise of the tormenting cough. Despite my best effort, I couldn't follow anything that was whispered around the cup. Watching the flame spark and die, seven times in a row, had a hypnagogic effect. Finally, Grandma sat down on the bed and handed me the cup.

"Here. Take three sips and ask the Powers who assisted in making this medicine to heal you." I looked first at the water in the cup, then at Grandma.

"What was the last sentence that you said after dousing the seventh match," I asked whispering carefully, to avoid triggering another bout of dry cough.

"Will you drink, please?"

"No. First you tell me that last sentence, and also promise to train me as a witch and a healer like yourself. Then I drink…" I burst into hacking, my chest burning with lacerating pain. Grandma grabbed the cup from my hands afraid that it would spill all over the blanket. It hurt so badly that it made tears run down my cheeks. Yet I tightened my lips as Grandma brought the cup closer to my mouth. I sustained her gaze, and my head – with a will of its own – turned firmly left to right. Mine was a definite no. Another bout of cough, more pain, and more tears. Another no to Grandmother's attempt to persuade me into drinking.

"By the powers of the Fierce Ones, by the powers of the Holy Ones, by the powers of the Bright Ones I banish this disease. Cough shall vanish as darkness vanishes with the rising of the morning sun. The new day shall find Daniela healed from this ailment; may she rise up to vibrant health, fresh like spring flowers in the field," said Grandma in one breath. "And yes, I will teach you. Have it your way. Now, drink."

My jaw dropped. I took the cup from her hands, and asked the Powers – whatever powers Grandma had invoked in the making of that charm – to heal me. I took three slow sips, and felt the solemnity of the moment. Each time I had had a chance to sneak in or somehow participate in Grandma's workings, I had always felt that sense of holiness arising from her words and gestures, and permeating the space around us.

I had nothing else to wish for. Oh, that wasn't true: I wished to get well as quickly as possible to begin my real apprenticeship. Afraid that I'll forget the charm, I picked up a notebook and pen from the nightstand, and wrote it down quickly. I pushed the notebook and pen under the pillow, slid down under the covers, and rolled over. I felt carried away on some giant wings, floating, sliding through thick mists, wind brushing against my cheeks and ruffling my hair. From afar, I heard Ms. Constanza saying something about a soothing hot drink and something to eat, but I dropped into nothingness.

Chapter 5

Within a couple of hours after waking up, I knew that the cough was gone for good. My throat and the inside of my chest felt as if they'd been rubbed with broken glass though. Even breathing felt painful. But the cough was gone and I couldn't have been any happier and grateful. Whatever powers Grandma asked for help, I lavishly expressed my gratitude by pouring out for them more than half of the milk and chocolate that was part of my breakfast. I barely had finished drinking the rest when the door opened and Grandma walked in. I could tell that something made her unhappy.

"Good morning, Princess," she spoke before I could open my mouth to say something. "Even if the milk and chocolate is not of your liking, you still shouldn't throw it out the window."

"Good morning, Grandma. I didn't throw away the milk. I poured an offering to the Powers. I'm not allowed to go outside yet, so I opened the window and poured it out for Them."

Grandma gave me a sharp look. "Who showed you how to do this?"

"Yourself. I saw you pouring out milk, water, wine, and beer. I remember you and the ladies leaving food outside, near the big beech tree in the woods…"

"How do you know about the food?" Grandma didn't even try to hide her surprise.

"I, umm, followed you once. Maybe twice. But you never told me who the Powers are. Do they have names? Was the lady in your room one of them?"

"Nothing escapes you, right? You'll get your answers, all in due time," Grandma said, finishing to braid my hair.

"But you promise to teach me if I drink the water. I did drink it, so now it is your turn to…." Slightly raising the voice brought tears to my eyes: my throat was still so raw.

"I promised to teach you, but I didn't say when I was going to begin."

That had the effect of a bucketful of cold water dumped on my head. The dream, at my fingertips only moments ago, slipped farther away. I must have looked deplorable, because Grandma put a hand on my shoulder in a comforting gesture.

"Remember what we talked about when you came to my room," she said. "You do your part, and I'll do mine. And don't worry about your parents. If you promise to keep your mouth shut and not give into anger anymore, I'll find a way around."

I nodded. The cloud lifted off my heart and probably off my face too. Grandma smiled.

I raised my hand for probably the tenth time, and finally summoning up my courage I knocked at the door.

"Come in," came the answer.

I walked in and greeted Grandma who wanted to know about my day at school. I had been able to stay out of trouble, and despite having missed a few days, my grades did not take a beating, as my parents feared they would.

I was embarrassed to ask, but I went on asking anyway:

"Um, how is Marius doing? Is it true that he had a second surgery?"

"How do you know about the second surgery?"

"Kids were talking at school. They were saying that when the car hit him, he broke both his right shin bone and thigh bone. And that he needed another surgery for his hip because the bone wasn't set properly the first time."

I sighed. I really felt bad for Marius. He had been on my mind for a while, and I was questioning my own avoidance to go visit him.

"Does he know that I cursed him?"

"What? Of course not. Unless you told someone, neither Marius, nor his Grandma, nor your parents know about this."

My heart felt suddenly light as a feather.

"I guess I should go visit him," I said. "Would you come with me, please?"

I was uncomfortable facing anybody in their family.

"Listen here: don't give yourself too much credit for that curse, ok? That accident could have happened even without your intervention. Let's put this to rest once and for all."

"Of course. But, are you coming with me?"

Marius's mom opened the door. She was surely glad to see Grandma, but winced when her eyes met mine. I wondered what exactly Marius told her about our encounters. We took off our winter coats and boots, and followed her into Marius' room. His grandmother was with him. Grandma poked me in the back. I followed exactly the instructions she gave me before leaving the house: flowers to Marius's grandmother and the chocolate box to him. Seeing Marius's face when I gave him the chocolate, wishing him to get well soon, was priceless. The moment I dreaded the most, arrived. Both ladies walked out the room leaving Marius and me alone. I realized that I had made a hole in my sweater by nervously tugging at a thread. I cursed. Marius laughed. I turned and picked up a deck of cards off the nightstand and shook it to make the cards rattle. "Wanna play?"

I had heard that Marius was an excellent player. Cards, board games, anything that was a strategy game – Marius was the master of it. I had no illusion to beat him, yet I had chosen to play cards. Was it a pretty desperate attempt that I made to patch the uncomfortable silence? Was I still guilt-ridden, despite Grandma's reassurance about the spell I had cast, and willing to do some form of penance? Anyway, Marius won in the most authoritative manner, beating the daylights out of me at pretty much everything that we played. Well, except for backgammon where the dice favored me.

Our grandmothers walked in. I did not realize that an hour and a half had gone by.

"It was good to see you, and I really hope you'll be on your feet soon." I said my line exactly as I had rehearsed it. The whole situation felt terribly awkward. Marius was awkward. I wasn't sure which version of him I felt more comfortable with. I guess I had become so accustomed to dealing with the bully that the mild-mannered boy making casual conversation over games felt completely unnatural. I took a step backwards toward the door. Marius stretched out his arm for a handshake. I felt my eyes narrowing slightly: was he putting up the good-boy-show to impress our grandmothers? I had no choice but to get closer and shake hands.

"Thanks for coming. If you have time after school tomorrow, do you want to come over? I didn't show you my stamp collection."

I nodded and left as quickly as I could. I couldn't shake off the belief that if there was one single big villain to be found in the whole world, that was me.

Marius's mother opened the door and ushered me in. But differently from the day before when she had winced upon seeing me, Mrs. Demeter greeted me with a smile. Astonished by the unexpectedly warm welcome, I tripped over the threshold. The books I held under my arm scattered on the hallway floor. Marius's mom helped me pick them up. She paused, holding up the heftiest book.

"The Vikings", she said. "F.G Bengtsson? Did you read this? It's not at all a children's book."

I nodded vigorously, and explained that I believed Marius would like it too. That particular book, 'The Vikings', was one of the things that I treasured the most, and it took Grandma some time to convince me to lend it to Marius.

"Don't be afraid to share with him the books that you love. You only risk turning an enemy into a friend," were Grandma's words.

"What if he's back being a bully as soon as he gets well?"

"But what if he doesn't?"

Anyway, there I was walking toward Marius' room. About halfway up the stairs, Mrs. Demeter stopped and turned to face me.

"Daniela, I must ask you for a favor."

My eyes widened. Mrs Demeter asking me for a favor? Feeling speechless, I nodded quickly.

Marius's mother sighed, then whispered so only I could hear:

"Marius is afraid he'll never walk properly again. He's afraid his leg, the one with the surgeries, will never heal. Could you please encourage him a little?"

"But is this true?" I felt horrified. I remembered briefly the moment I cursed him, my own words, "your bones will break, Marius," and I had to hold onto the banister, feeling suddenly lightheaded.

Misunderstanding my reaction, Mrs. Demeter hugged me. Her voice quivered as she spoke.

"One of the orthopedics believes so, and Marius overheard the conversation." I sniffled, and blinked quickly. Still hugging me, Mrs. Demeter continued: "I never thought that despite your bickering you could actually be such a good friend to him. Thank you, dear child!"

I wanted to scream.

"Hi! I can't wait to see your stamp collection." I faked a cheerful voice. In response, Marius forced a smile. "And I have something I thought you may love to read," I added, and with a theatrical gesture, I showcased 'The Vikings'. "I also brought you 'Robin Hood' and 'The Weasel Brothers'".[3]

"Are you being nice just because you know that I won't be able to walk again? Are you pitying me? I don't need your pity nor anyone else's!" Marius shouting made me feel at ease: that was the normal tone for all our previous conversations after all. I leaped near his bed, and holding the stacked books up directly over his injured leg, I shouted back:

"Say that shit again and I'm dropping these right onto your leg. Then you'll have a real reason to believe that you won't be walking again. I have no pity for you, why should I? I was in a wheelchair for almost four months, and when I could barely walk you made fun of me. Walky-ducky, remember?" Oops! The last part came out without me intending for it, and I became concerned about how Marius would react. What was I going to tell Mrs. Demeter if that was to escalate into an argument?

"I knew you had been in a wheelchair, but I didn't mean to make fun of you. I wanted to make a joke, and thought that maybe, just once, we could talk without fighting. I didn't know that you can't tell apart a joke from an insult. Do you feel better now? Do you feel avenged?"

So, Grandma was right all along. Even if I could blame Marius for being the bully in ninety percent of the cases, there was still another ten percent when he was not. It was my faulty assumption that made him the bad guy one hundred percent of the time.

"I'm sorry Marius. I really am." I was being honest. "I don't care about any revenge. I'm really looking forward to seeing you well again." That was only half true: while I was sorry and, additionally, harbored some guilt, I was also glad that Marius gained some insight into my own suffering. Of course, I was not going to reveal that part of my thoughts to him.

"Listen, don't let anyone tell you that you won't be able to walk again. I know that you will be back on your feet. Really. I'll help you, ok?" Initially, I didn't know how I could actually help, but as soon as those words left my mouth, an idea took shape in my mind.

Marius smiled, genuinely that time. He pointed to the bookshelf: "Third shelf from the bottom, all the way to your right. The two blue binders: that's my stamp collection. Bring it over here... please."

I burst into the kitchen, panting so hard I couldn't even speak. As soon as I got my breath back, I blurted out: "Grandma, I am sure you can help Marius heal. Please Grandma!"

There was no one else in the kitchen besides us.

"Did you offer Marius any help that involves me and, uh... any old ways or remedies?"

"No. I promised you once that I'll be very careful about what I say and to whom. But I told Marius that I would help him." Then I gave an account of the discussions I had with Mrs. Demeter and with Marius himself.

"Hmmm, easier said than done, dear child." I raised my eyebrows, being both curious and incredulous. No healing feat was too hard for Grandma or Mrs. Constanza: they helped my legs heal, and I saw no reason they could not do the same for Marius. Grandma answered my thoughts:

"Marius' grandfather is a retired priest[4], and has a very firm position against many of the folk healing practices. He believes that if it is not done by a priest or inside the church, healing powers come from darker powers." Grandma rolled her eyes, and continued to explain." And Marius' parents themselves are, ummm..., very much like your father: they don't believe in anything outside conventional medicine." I smirked, because Grandma had been a nurse in the surgery ward for almost thirty years before retiring. Heck, she understood the medical field! Grandma held in high regard both modern and folk medicine. As far as where she was getting her powers and knowledge from,

I believed that it was no one's business. She helped people, and that alone should have mattered, nothing else.

"I must talk to Marius' grandmother, and see what can be done. Good job, Daniela, really good job."

She turned around to turn off the oven and took out a tray of freshly baked muffins. The aroma filled the kitchen: my mouth turned into an artesian fountain, and I heard my stomach growling. I poured myself a glass of milk and carefully removed a couple of muffins from the tray and sat them on a plate.

"Just those two," said Grandma, "Don't touch the tray again. Your mom would have a fit to see you eating muffins before dinner. Glad she's not around. I'm going to call Amelia." I sighed with relief, knowing that Grandma would speak with Marius' grandmother right away. I was sure that the two of them would come up with a plan.

Chapter 6

After having examined me, the doctor asked to talk to my mother alone. I was asked to wait outside in the lobby. The psychologist who evaluated me was my mother's colleague. They both worked in the same clinic, just in different departments. Once outside the doctor's office, I lowered myself onto a chair in the waiting area but as soon as the door closed behind my mother, I stood up quickly like my legs were made of springs. I was the only one in the lobby, so... My ear flattened itself against the door, pushing vehemently against the white-painted wood smelling of antiseptic. Nothing. Then, there was the noise of drawers opening and closing followed by the clinging of cups and teaspoons: are they having coffee? What in the world? I quickly reviewed, mentally, the discussion I just had with the doctor. I couldn't find any flaws. I had followed exactly Grandma's instructions. "You are not smart enough if you cannot play ignorant when circumstances require," Grandma had told me when I hesitated about denying my experiences.

She insisted that I should not tell the doctor that I was seeing colors, hearing music, and occasionally seeing things that no one else other than myself could see. Grandma explained to me that there were people affected by serious pathologies, who were also seeing and hearing things in hallucinatory experiences. That was a serious concern. I could have been wrongly diagnosed with some mental illness. Grandmother reassured me that it was not my case. She explained that almost all my ancestresses, herself included, had the gift of seeing as she named it. She also explained to me that medicine people, fairy seers, witches, can harness their abilities and use them as needed while the unfortunate ones who dealt with pathologies, could not. I sighed with relief, glad to know that I wasn't just a "deranged" child as Comrade Caran insinuated, but I actually had a gift as I had wished the case to be.

"Lia," the doctor said addressing Mother by her first name, "the child is fine. She is bored. She has a lot of energy, a sharp intellect, and the only thing she lacks is more physical exercise. I would recommend swimming. Daniela told me that she used to skate and you made her quit. Do you know how much she's still suffering? Allow her to have something in exchange for what is being taken away from her, and she'll have other things on her mind rather than pretending that she has magical powers."

"But she is so frail! She may get ill again if I were to let her swim. And sports would take away from the time she needs to study…"

"Lia, you are not helping her." The doctor interrupted my mom's frantic and disjointed attempt to argue her choices, her decision to keep me in the little box that she had created for me and where I had to be squelched to please her. In Mother's opinion, sports were not ladylike, therefore I should have not been encouraged toward any. Ice skating, that she had stopped me brutally from pursuing, was, in her opinion, too dangerous. Had the doctor suggested for me to join a knitting or a drawing club, she'd have signed me up in the blink of an eye. "Sign her up for dance classes. It's the closest thing to skating, minus the danger of falling or catching colds. And it's very well suited for a girl, if Daniela being a tomboy, is your concern."

I imagined myself taking dance and archery lessons, and the very thought of the possibility made me giddy. I wanted to jump up and down, and maybe do some cartwheels. I would have been happy with any of the doctor's suggestions. I heard Mother muttering something about vitamins and minerals that I should be taking because I was so thin, that sports would exhaust me too much, and that they would take away from my study time. The doctor interrupted her again.

"Lia, we have known each other for over twenty years. Don't you think that in addition to being a childhood psychologist, having raised three kids of my own qualifies me enough to advise what's suitable for Daniela? She's at the top of her class, and on every single test I administered she scored far above her age. You are overreacting. Don't rob Daniela of her childhood and kill her dreams. Please."

I heard papers rustling, then the doctor speaking again.

"Here's the paperwork from the assessment that I conducted on her today. To lay to rest your worries and those of the teacher, I also wrote a referral for a neurologist to do a check-up. I refuse at this point to send her for a psychiatric evaluation, I don't care what that teacher says. If you ask me, I'll move Daniela to a different teacher, different classroom, or different school altogether. She's being traumatized enough. This is not even a ten-year-old child that we are talking about."

I moved farther back, and made sure that the door opening would yield to the sight of me practicing cartwheels and pirouettes. "What did I tell you?" the doctor said, pointing in my direction. "Really Lia, get her into dancing."

Nor the psychological evaluation, nor the neurologist's examination made Comrade Caran change her attitude toward me. The neurologist's statement that I was perfectly healthy, added to the psychologist's report about my cognitive development, actually made my classroom teacher even more resentful.

"It means that you are a liar, and that you are making fun of us," Comrade Caran shouted at me, ignoring that both my parents were present.

"We have decided to transfer Daniela to a different teacher, and we are here to talk to the principal," Father said coldly. "And personally, I am not interested to hear your opinion on my daughter."

Comrade Caran paused for a moment, her jaw hanging, then probably aware of the comic display that she offered, snapped her mouth closed, turned on her heels, and stormed out the room[5]. We were soon ushered into the office of the principal, and half an hour later, the principal herself accompanied me to Comrade Moisa's room. My new teacher, who, obviously, was prepared for my arrival, introduced me to the class, and, to my greatest joy, had me seated in the first row near the front of the room.

For the rest of the day, I directed my efforts at making a great impression on the teacher, and making friends among the kids in my class. As I trotted through snow on the way home, I thought of how my Trojan Horse was growing. Then I realized that I was growing alongside my Trojan Horse. The "horse" I had imagined would get me into Grandma's citadel of well-guarded secrets was in fact accomplishing far more than this. I was becoming a little bit more popular. People seemed to 'discover' me, and I believed some even liked me. I felt happy, if only for a moment. The moment of joyful realization did not last. To stay out of trouble and make myself accepted, I spoke no more about fairies or other spirits, about my belief that they truly existed, nor about magic. I didn't show my upset – or outright sadness – whenever Grandma disappeared in her room with Mrs. Constanza or other ladies in her circle whenever they were coming over. I pretended that I did not resent Vica, who in her newly appointed position of guardian made sure that I wasn't getting anywhere near that room when Grandmother had her guests visiting. I began to question whether Grandma really had the intention to ever teach me anything. Maybe my parents convinced her not to, so she was actually trying to back out of our agreement without me noticing it. It would have never crossed my mind to think of it, except that I believed I recognized the pattern my parents used so many times before. Like allowing me to return to skating, or take horseback riding lessons: I was never told 'no' directly, but only promised that it'll happen at some point in the future, and then pointing out how all kind of 'obstacles' came in the way to delay it, so the whatever-it-was-that-I-wanted got pushed farther and farther back. When I ceased asking, my parents would then assume I had forgotten, and that the 'phase' was over. In my mind, however, nothing was forgotten.

Once home, I went straight to my room. It was no small surprise to find mother and Vica searching through drawers and shelves. My eyes fell on a box on the floor. At the sight of its contents, I panicked. I threw myself over the box: my fingers turned claws, grasped the notebook, the wand, and tried to do the same with one of the fairytales books thrown in there. Vica grabbed me by the arm and pulled me away. I squeezed my notebook and wand to my chest, decided to defend them whatever that meant. Both Mother and Vica advanced toward me.

"It is for your own good, Daniela. One day you will understand." Mother stretched her hand out, demanding that I'd hand over the notebook, the one where I recorded all the little spells I made up and whatever else I could pick up from Grandma, and the wand – a pine twig that I had carved and decorated myself. I knew what that meant: whatever they'd take away from me it would be gone forever. I was determined not to let it happen. I took a step backwards in the direction of the door, but Vica, who was still clenching at my arm, pushed me sideways. With her free hand she grabbed the notebook.

"NOOOO!" I screamed. A slap landed over my cheek, and I heard Mother threatening to beat the daylights out of me if I wouldn't stop screaming. I filled up my lungs and screamed again, louder than before. The door burst open with so much force that it hit the wall. Grandma and Father rushed into the room. Lightning fast, I turned my head and bit Vica's hand as hard as I could. She screamed and relented the grip for one moment which was enough for me to get to the door. Grandma blocked the way.

"What's going on here?" Father had arrived home only moments ago and having heard the commotion, rushed to my room. Mother and Vica began to explain their reasons for purging my room. "Leave her books alone, " said Father. All of them." Then he turned toward me. "What are these? Can I see?"

I was shaking. "Please, Daddy..." As he tugged, I felt my treasured possessions slipping away from me as if life itself would slip away from someone who lost interest in it entirely. I needed a miracle. I closed my eyes." To the Powers who helped me heal, I call and beg for Your help. If any fairy beings are near, please help. Don't let my notebook and wand, especially the notebook, be taken away. I'll be your friend forever, I promise." I barely finished my thought, and as through enchantment I heard Grandma speak.

"Oh, I will take care of those." Like in slow motion, I saw my possessions changing hands. Then Grandma left the room. I did not know if that was a good or a bad thing. My notebook and wand were safe with Grandma, but once locked up in her room they would be lost to me anyway. I looked at my family through the curtain of tears blurring my eyes: a bunch of people violating my space and trampling over everything I cared about. Something broke within me in a way that I felt was beyond repair. I left the room unnoticed by the adults caught into a fervent argument.

"Come in," said Grandma as soon as she heard me knocking. My notebook, its covers crumpled, and my wand, laid on the table.

"It's good that tomorrow is Sunday. You can't show up to school frazzled like this. You need to calm down." Grandma stood up and disappeared in the bathroom. I heard the water running for a while, then she came out holding a small, wet towel. She applied the cold compress on my cheek. It hurt, but I didn't complain. I went on and told her what had just happened since she had no idea about Mother's plan to search my room and remove everything she believed had a bad influence on me. When I mentioned fighting back and biting Vica, Grandma gasped and covered her mouth, obviously displeased. "For now, your things will remain here with me. Until the storm passes."

I didn't trust a word of what she said, I didn't trust anyone in my family at that point, but I was too tired to argue. I left Grandma's room, and went straight to the cupboard in the kitchen downstairs. In less than one minute, four cups from Mother's favorite tea set and their accompanying saucers laid on the floor, in shards.

The intruders were gone. First thing that I did upon entering my room was to open all the windows. It made the room freezing cold, but I would rather freeze than feel Mother's perfume or Vica's perennial scent of cooked food lingering into the air I breathed. I wanted my room back. I wanted it to feel as it did before – a sanctuary where I always felt safe, where I could be myself, surrounded by my favorite books and toys, where I could dream and think of whatever I wanted. The feeling of safety was gone though, and the space didn't feel like a sanctuary either. I knelt by the box left on the floor and picked up the books. I patted the covers affectionately, and little by little I felt my heart warming up to the joy of having my fairy tales collection there, unscathed. I put the books back into the bookcase. I sat at my desk. I was glad to notice that the chair was in the exact same position I left it the night before: it meant that none of the perpetrators sat on it. They had searched my drawers though. I knew it because that was where they found my wand and notebook. I rearranged my things, pencils, pens, bottles of ink in different colors...the key from the top drawer was gone. So, if I ever wanted to keep something secret, I had to find a good hiding place. I looked around. Vica dusted and mopped every week, so anything placed atop the shelves or under the bed would have been discovered. My school books were few, and anything placed between them would stand out. I began pacing the room. The painting hanging on the wall caught my eye. No one would ever search behind it. If I could only find a way to secure a notebook and wand between the painting and the wall! I made a mental note to investigate that possibility.

I had promised Marius to visit him, and I was almost running late. It was Saturday afternoon, and we had planned to watch 'Tarzan' on TV. I realized that even without the incentive that I had, to please Grandma in the hope that she'll finally make me her apprentice, I was genuinely glad to visit with Marius. He liked to read as much as I did, and we even enjoyed the same kind of books. We liked the same movies and the same games. Too bad that I couldn't mention anything magic, fairy, or witchy to him. Why couldn't we get along before the accident? Why did it take a tragedy to happen for us to become friends? But were we really friends? I meant, was this friendship going to last once he'd be walking again?

I washed my face, combed my hair, changed clothes and dumped my school uniform into the laundry hamper. On my way out, I left the hamper by the door so Vica would have no reason to enter my room at least for some time. I was about to close the door behind me when I realized that the door key was also gone. Anger choked me. They were planning therefore to rob me of the last bit of privacy! I turned back, opened one of the drawers at my desk and grabbed a piece of paper. I furiously tore it into tiny pieces –- maybe the very act of tearing or breaking acted in itself as an outlet for the anger that I felt. I called onto the Powers whose names I didn't know, yet whose presence I could clearly sense, to grant me revenge. I wanted for the adults in my house to experience as much discomfort, fear, pain, anger, and humiliation as I did. No, I wanted them to feel at least twice as much as I felt in the past few hours. I scattered the bits of paper on my desk and shuffled them with my hands while intently asking the Powers to teach my family a lesson. I finally stood up to leave. A gust of wind made the curtains swell, and blew the bits of paper all over the room. I closed the windows, and ran downstairs. I'd still be in time to watch 'Tarzan' with Marius.

Chapter 7

I found Marius frazzled, his mom and both grandparents gathered around him. He quickly wiped his eyes with his sleeve, embarrassed to be seen crying. I found out that he had appointments with both the orthopedic and the physical therapist, and despite his best efforts during the session, Marius was still not making any progress. Did Grandma talk with Marius' grandmother? I had no idea. I reassured Marius that he would walk. I wasn't lying and I wasn't trying to give him false hope; somehow, I knew that he would walk again, and even ride his bike. I told him and all those gathered around us that I was very well acquainted with the struggle he was facing, having been there myself. Five pairs of eyes devoured hungrily every syllable I uttered. I answered Mr. Demeter's questions, and explained that following a mismanaged medical incident I ended up with my legs ankylosed from hips down and for a while I moved around in a wheelchair. I told her about the exercises I did while actually sitting in the chair, some of them prescribed by my PT and some that I had invented out of boredom. Spurred on by the reactions of such a great audience, I almost got into talking about the work that Grandma did for me, sometimes alone and sometimes joined by other ladies. I stopped just on the cusp of saying too much. Sensing that I left my thoughts and words hanging in midair, Mr. Demeter encouraged me to continue.

"Please feel free to share with us everything about your healing journey, Daniela. It gives us all faith, and we all need it, Marius in particular."

But I was done. By no means was I going to tell anything more. Then, Marius and I were left alone to enjoy the movie.

"You said you had an idea about helping me. What was that about," Marius asked.

"Ummm…." I was forcing myself to think of something that did not involve Grandmother and her healing methods, although that was precisely what I had in mind when I had first mentioned helping Marius. "I don't know if you are up to it…" I said, bidding for time. Why in moments like that my brain would freeze?

"Come on, I promise I won't make fun of you no matter how silly your idea is."

There was a sudden spark in my mind.

"Ok… I was thinking, maybe, to come here every day and do the exercises with you, you know, show you the ones that your doc has prescribed, and also maybe weave in some of those things that I basically invented and which really helped me get off the wheel chair. I know that generally speaking, you don't really like to exercise, but with a buddy like myself that may be different." I had no idea how that thought came to my mind, but I was very pleased with what I said.

"Yeah, so you can be the boss, right?" And seeing my disappointed face, Marius burst into laughter. "Can you ever tell when someone is joking?" Then, seeing me relax, he continued: "Can't be any worse than it is right now. I'm getting tired of listening to my classmates, who talk about nothing but snowball fights and going sledding every day after school. Ok, Coach. Let's tell my dad."

Part of me wanted to rush home, to tell Grandma about my new role as "Coach". I was also eager to ask whether she had already talked to Marius' grandmother about doing some healing for him. The other part of me didn't rush so much, reluctant to face Mother. I began to think that destroying half of her favorite tea set hadn't been the best idea. I walked in just in time for dinner. To my surprise, the atmosphere was calm as if nothing had ever happened. I washed my hands, sat down, and once Vica brought the food to the table I began to tuck in. Father broke the silence:

"Congratulations," he addressed me, raising his glass in my direction. "Comrade Moisa called us to tell that you are at the top of the class. She praised you highly for the knowledge you have about Romanian folk traditions and heritage[6]. She also told us that you will be the youngest student on the team representing the school in a history and culture-themed contest which is scheduled in spring."

Father poured wine for everyone and filled my glass with sparkling water.

"Cheers to Daniela!" Everyone raised the glass.

I guess I forgot to chew. So, my fairy tales and folklore collection that Mother wanted to purge earlier that day turned out to be an asset for my education. I found the irony absolutely delightful.

Surprisingly enough, no one mentioned anything about the torn bits of paper littering my room, nor about the broken tea cups. The discussion turned toward my newly formed friendship with Marius. Over the almost three years since they had moved into their house, the Demeter family and mine never interacted much, except for the old Mrs. Demeter, Marius grandmother, and my own grandmother who became very close to each other since the day they first met. I was quite glad to share about Marius and me turning into friends from previously sworn enemies. Mother was beaming at me, and even tried to pat me on the head. When she raised her hand, I instinctively jerked and closed my eyes, the memory of the slap I had received from her earlier still too fresh to put behind. I relaxed quickly though, and Mother touched my head gently, whispering so I would be the only one to hear:

"I am so sorry for earlier. I really am. I wish it didn't come to …"

Mother didn't find the words to finish the sentence. I was also lacking the words to tell how I really felt about it, so I simply nodded. Over the years, I had gotten used to Mother's mood changing on the spur of the moment. However, that was the first time ever she'd slapped me, and that thing alone was telling me that something else was going on, something that made Mother even more emotionally labile than usual. I discreetly looked at my parents to see whether they were still at odds with each other or made peace in the aftermath of the incident that took place in my room earlier that afternoon. I sighed with relief: at least apparently, the tension between them had passed like a summer thunderstorm.

After dinner, I left my parents seated by the fire with the usual Saturday night, after-dinner glass of wine. Vica was washing the dishes, and only muttered something unintelligible in response to me telling everyone goodnight. Grandmother nudged me to follow her into her room.

As soon as the door closed behind us, Grandma asked, "What were the bits of paper scattered all over in your room? Fortunately, I walked in right after you left and cleaned everything before anyone else saw anything."

"Thank you, Grandma, but why did you go into my room?" I was curious what her answer would be to that.

"Well, " said grandma with biting sarcasm in her voice, I just happened to come upon your mother and Vica debating over who broke the teacups and left the china shards laying on the floor. I told them that I broke them by mistake while trying to reach past, to get something from farther back on the shelf. I was just about to clean up the mess – this is what I told them. I thought I'd take a look at your room also, and I'm glad that I did. It has been my full-time job today to clean the mess you left behind."

How lucky was I! Having Grandma always come to my rescue, that in itself was a magical gift in its own right. I thanked her wholeheartedly, but then I had to explain both the broken cups and the scattered bits of paper. More uncomfortable than talking about the incidents was for me to admit that I acted in anger. Grandma listened patiently.

"And how am I supposed to trust you with more magic when you act so destructively when getting angry? What if, in your fit of anger, without even knowing, you have invited bad things to happen to your family by tearing and scattering the bits of paper in what seems to me revenge spell-casting? I'm not saying that it will happen with certainty, but when you ask for magical powers, you must handle your emotions carefully. You cannot release your anger as spells and curses just as you did with Marius, remember?"

"But how can I not get angry when I am being mistreated? How can I not be angry when Mother barges into my room and begins to throw away my things? How can I not be angry when she opposes almost everything that I want to do?"

"You may get angry, of course. I would be angry with people trying to take away from me what I love, or push me into being something that I am not. But you do not have to be destructive in your anger!" Grandma raised her voice slightly to make sure she got her point across.

Breaking something or cursing made my anger go away, but Grandma expected me to refrain from doing any of those. I thought that even if there would be any repercussions, I should not be sorry: whoever crossed me, incurred the wrath of the Powers[7] I called. Right? But...Cursing Marius, whether that really did have an effect or not, didn't bring me any satisfaction, quite the opposite. I began to feel a little uneasy about the impromptu curse I launched myself into earlier, when I had wished so fervently for my parents to taste the bitterness that I was tasting. I kept those thoughts to myself though. I asked Grandma:

"And what exactly am I supposed to do when I am angry?"

"I'll teach you a spell for anger. It also works for fears."

I was all ears. I bet my eyes were sparkling, and I was probably holding my breath. This was so unexpected. Grandma held my hands and looked me in the eyes.

"When you get angry, you get pen and paper, and you write down as much as you can about what or who makes you angry. Pour out your anger on paper. Then you tear the paper into small pieces, drop it in the toilet, and flush it down the drain. You can also throw the pieces into the trash can, and then take the trash out. Will your anger be gone, so your mind can clear. Understood?"

"So... whoever hurts me goes unpunished, and I shall be ok, and maybe they will try to do the same again, and all I have to do is just flush my anger in the toilet ...I don't understand how this is supposed to make me feel good."

Grandma sighed.

"If you get rid of anger, you can think clearly. When you are not angry, you don't seek revenge. If you don't seek revenge and don't focus on how to pay back the wrongdoer, you can focus instead on how to solve the problem that you actually care about solving. You could think of actions you can take to prevent others from doing things that upset you. You may decide to break even with them at some point, but plan on it when you are not angry and when you can think properly. Anger destroyed your aunt's life. She was never able to move past her anger, and thought of exacting revenge more than of solving the actual problems she faced." Grandma paused and let go of my hands. "I may be asking too much of you. You are just a child and I am assigning you to a task where a grownup woman, Aunt Camelia, failed. Not giving in to anger. Hmmm. Not sure if I should expect you to even try."

I felt challenged by Grandma's doubtful words.

"Of course, I can do this," I said. "Now can I have my notebook and wand back?"

"Not yet. I want to see that you really can control yourself when you get angry. I also don't want to fall short on the promise I made to your parents..." Grandma left the sentence unfinished. She looked away. I had another question for her.

"Grandma, could you think of a way to help Marius? I will do PT exercises with him, but without your healing I'm not sure how much progress he will actually make."

"Leave that up to me, and do not worry. I talked to Amelia, and we have a plan. It may be the case that Marius' grandfather shall never know about it, or at least not until the poor child is back on his feet. You don't say a word to anybody, understood?"

Chapter 8

I heard the key turning in the door lock at Grandma's room. I thought enviously that Grandma was about to have friends coming over and they'll do rituals, divination, and probably some of the magic that I had been banned from even watching. I was dying to know who would come to visit and for what purpose. However, the dark, massive door – an impassable guardian that would not yield to any pleas or negotiation attempts – blocked my way. I felt anger rising. "STOP!" I bellowed in my head, and took a deep breath. There was no time to do any anger, banishing the way Grandma had taught me a couple of days ago, so I just yelled at my anger to stop it from pushing through. It worked. I felt immensely powerful. I relaxed a little at the thought that if I still needed to, I could do an anger-releasing ritual later, at my own convenience. What did Grandma say? Oh, right. When the mind is clear I can think of solutions to whatever I need to solve. I didn't have time to lament over the door being in my way; I should look for a window instead. So, a minute or so later I was downstairs, locked up in the half bathroom, standing on the rim of the toilet. I felt my toes like the claws of an eagle, grasping at the cold porcelain to help me balance in that precarious position. I could only reach high enough to see through the lower third of the bathroom window. From my position I could see who was coming to visit grandmother. To walk through the separate entrance that led to Grandma's quarters, visitors had to pass right by me.

Seeing the last two of Grandma's guests nearly made me lose my balance; none other than Marius' own mother and grandmother walked in! As soon as they all walked inside, I left my strategic position and ran upstairs. The massive, impossible guardian, could block my sight, but could not prevent me from hearing the secrets it was meant to hide. I laid my belly down on the thick carpet in the corridor. Propped up on my elbows, I glued my right ear to the bottom of the door. No one coming upstairs could see me, unless they were to go to my parents' bedroom which was about fifteen feet away and diagonally across from Grandma's. I breathed deeply and slowly, trying to still my heart. Because of the pounding in my chest, I couldn't hear anything across the door. Finally, I relaxed a little, and curiosity took over nervousness. I felt on the verge of some amazing discovery.

I heard the usual greetings exchange. Then, judging from the noises, everyone sat down. Someone walked around, murmuring something I could not understand.

"Let's see what you have," Grandma said.

"Here's the T-shirt Marius slept with, the hair and the nail clippings." I recognized the voice of Miss Amelia, Marius' grandmother. "I feel terrible that I have to hide this from my husband and my son, but I have to help the poor child, and this is the last thing to try, the last hope…" Miss Amelia's voice broke, and I heard her sobbing. Aside from the sobs, the only sound breaking the silence was the rustling noise made by someone searching around for something. Then I heard Grandmother's voice, again:

"Here. Yes, you cut it like this. And you stuff inside more cloth, the hair, and the nail clippings. Then we'll name the doll. Let's take care of this once and for all. Amelia, this worked for Daniela, and I have no doubt that will work for Marius. Have a little faith in our work and power. And, you know, this is a secret. First, the fewer people talk about and know about it, the more power it has. Second, if the word somehow spreads outside these circles, we may all land in jail. Aside from my own daughter and Vica, whom I both trust, nobody knows we gather and do our…thing. There was a time, not too long ago when we were not afraid to help other people with readings and a little bit of hands-on healing, the kind we are just about to do for Marius. But nowadays we are more and more guarded and don't receive anyone from the outside anymore. We practice our skills mostly among ourselves because we want to practice. You know, once someone is on this path, they are forever on this path."

Something didn't add up in my mind. Then I heard Marius' mother voicing the very question that I had.

"How is this going to work when Marius is not with us in the room?"

"It has his nails clippings and hair, and the t-shirt was in close contact with him through the night. Then there is you, his mother, and your presence and desire for him to heal lends strength to the work. You don't have to be convinced of the efficiency, but just consider that your willingness to try wholeheartedly is enough to raise power. It is like collective prayer. You'll see."

Grandma spoke with such confidence, that personally I had no doubt Marius' problems were already on their way to ending. I concentrated on memorizing what I had learned so far: a little doll made from cloth that touched the patient's body, stuffed with more of the same cloth plus a bit of their hair and nails clippings. I had no idea though how they were going to use the doll exactly.

Then, Grandmother stated out loud that the doll would take on Marius' identity, and whatever healing the doll received it would take effect simultaneously in Marius' body. I memorized almost every word, and felt ecstatic, despite my elbows becoming numb and my neck hurting. Unfortunately, for several minutes afterwards, I heard nothing but silence occasionally interrupted by the sound of someone or something moving. I had no idea how much time elapsed until Grandma's voice sounded again loud and clear.

"Ladies, bring your hand over Marius, here present with us – I assumed it was the doll she was referring to – and in whatever form you wish, ask whatever Power that you believe in, to grant this child healing so he may stand up and walk."

I had the beginning and the end of the healing ritual. I missed the middle part of it, and still didn't know what powers Grandma called on for healing. From my part, I cared more about what exactly she did with the doll from the moment she named it until the collective prayers were said. As far as the identity of the mysterious Powers, it could wait. I envisioned myself conducting healing rituals and calling, "To all the Powers that my Grandmother calls upon, I am asking for Your help." That should do. I had to write everything down as soon as possible.

Again, people shuffled around. Then Grandma said to Mrs. Amelia, "Take this and sprinkle it around Marius' room. Then for three nights soak a piece of cloth into it, and dab all over the injured leg."

What that was, I could not tell, but I imagined it must be some kind of liquid. I heard sniffling, words of gratitude, and Marius' mother asking how could she ever repay Grandma for her kindness. In response, Grandma chuckled and answered that she felt rewarded and even overpaid just by seeing how Marius and I get along and our families getting closer.

"Good friends are a rarity. Good neighbors can also be rare. But good neighbors who are also good friends are extremely rare." Everyone laughed.

I rolled away from the door and then jumped to my feet; there were steps coming in my direction. I bolted toward my parents' bedroom and disappeared inside as Grandmother opened the door and called out for Vica to bring coffee and cookies for the guests. When Grandma went back inside, I headed to my room and, in a hurry, jotted down on paper everything I could remember from the healing ritual. I used loose leaf paper instead of a notebook. Then I rolled the carpet until it uncovered about a third of the floor. I placed the sheets of paper closer to the center of the room, and then unrolled the carpet back. I had calculated that I could hide a good deal of notes that way, because as opposed to a single notebook, the loose-leaf paper could be scattered and wouldn't appear bulky through the rug. I still had to figure out a way to make a hiding place behind the painting on the wall across my desk, a little hideaway to store a small notebook.

From time to time, I went to check on Grandma's guests. When it became clear that they were about to leave, I ran to the "Observatory" – the bathroom downstairs but under a more glorifying name. I saw Marius' grandmother and his mother leaving, but whatever Grandma gave them to sprinkle around Marius' room and put on his leg was probably kept in one of their handbags because I could not see anything. I thought that, with a little bit of luck, when I'd go to Marius' house again, maybe I'll see the recipient.

I was comfortably installed in one of the armchairs in Grandma's room. Grandmother had asked whether I'd like to spend the afternoon with her. I wouldn't go to see Marius until the next day, and I had no plans to meet any of the new friends that I made since moving to Comrade Moisa's classroom, so, there I was, nibbling on cookies and sipping hot milk and coffee in Grandma's company. We began playing cards, but the conversation inevitably turned toward Marius. Grandma told me that his mother and grandmother came to see her.

"I know," I said without thinking much. "I saw them coming in, I mean, I was downstairs when they arrived, and saw them coming in."

"I did healing for Marius, and I need you to pretend that you saw nothing, know nothing, and not utter a word. His father and grandfather must not hear a word – they are a little bit against all these… you know."

"How can you heal someone who is not present?" I hoped that my question would prompt grandma to teach me about working with the doll.

"Well, you know very well how curses work, don't you?"

I nodded, but that was not at all the answer that I expected.

"Well, healing someone who is not present is like putting a curse on them, only that instead of wishing something ill and directing anger or hatred in their direction, one can direct love, kindness, and concentrate on healing instead of harming."

"And how exactly do you do this? Just think of the person you want to heal and send them loving thoughts and healing?

"That is the main idea, but the healer does far more than this. The healer makes a doll, and it is the doll that carries the energy of the person who receives the healing work. The doll itself is made from cloth that has been in direct contact with the receiver's body, and it also contains nail clippings and hair from the person who receives the healing. You see, there is a thread, invisible but immensely powerful, that connects the doll to the patient, so working on one affects the other. The person who is making the doll, and all those gathered for the healing session must pray and focus intently their thoughts and energies for this thing to work." She barely finished the sentence, and I jumped in:

"And what about the Powers? You called on Powers when you did healing on me. Did you also call them to help Marius? Who are they?"

"I'll teach you one day. When the time's right."

If there was one sentence in the whole world that I had grown deeply averse to, it was exactly the one that Grandma had just uttered. What did she mean by "the time being right"? What other conditions was I supposed to meet for her to teach me what she knew and reveal the mystery surrounding those Powers? So, I asked her, plain and simple, at which she answered:

"You have to be at least twelve years old to be initiated in this tradition, learn who the Powers are, and how to work alongside them. So, you have some waiting ahead of you," Grandma said.

"But you told me that your own grandmother, Cassandra, initiated you – whatever that means – when you were eleven because she saw that you were ready. This is what you said to me."

"Yes, some girls are ready sooner than others. It is a belief among healers like ourselves. When a girl's body transforms and advances toward womanhood, she's ready to know about the Powers and begin to work with them. You'll get to learn about it in due time, as I said..."

"Are you talking about menstruation? It's discussed in the fifth-grade biology book. Is this the big secret?" I would have been somewhat disappointed if so much fuss had been made around a normal biological function.

"Fifth grade book? You are still in third grade if I am not mistaken," Grandma said in a mocking tone.

"Marius lets me read all of his schoolbooks, and the stuff they learn in fifth grade is grand! I can't wait."

"Oh well, children nowadays... But speaking of the initiation into fai... into the kind of healing that is our tradition, well, it is a coming-of-age ritual. In that ritual you would be presented to the Powers, and you officially become an apprentice. So, you have to wait until your age, eleven or twelve or whatever that may be, will qualify you to become a, uh, healer like myself and your ancestresses."

"Uh...You said I must be of age to apprentice officially. But I can apprentice unofficially before that, right?"

"I believe that I told you enough. At least for a while."

Grandma sighed. I put the empty cup away, and suddenly became aware of the cookie turned mush into my sweaty palm. I had completely forgotten about it. Upon noticing, Grandma laughed. I felt encouraged by her good mood.

"Can I ask you..."

"No."

"Please, just one tiny thing," I insisted, and before Grandma giving any sign of either approval or dismissal, I continued. "What did you give Mrs. Demeter to sprinkle around Marius' room?" Before I finished asking, I regretted it already. How was I supposed to tell Grandma that I was eavesdropping? It was obviously too late to retract anything. Why couldn't I keep my mouth shut?

"So, you listened at the door." Grandma sounded resigned and mildly annoyed, but not angry. I took it as a good sign.

"I was passing by and heard voices, so I ..."

Grandma looked me straight into the eyes:

"Whatever. Make sure you don't breathe to anyone a single word about what you heard; do you understand? Absolutely to no one. This includes Marius himself."

I nodded several times feeling slightly nervous. Taking note of my reaction, Grandma went on:

"I shall teach you how to do that kind of water. It would be good for you to learn how to clean your room and yourself of anger and of anything of this sort that may be clinging onto you. In Marius' case, it was to remove the spirit of whatever is stuck onto him, slowing down healing and most importantly, undermining his confidence in himself. Come here now."

No words could have described my joy. I had eyes for nothing else other than Grandma's hands opening the dresser's doors. I had ears for nothing else other than every word she would utter. Grandma took out a bottle with some water in it. Then, one by one, she pulled out three bunches of dried herbs wrapped in brown paper. From a drawer, she took a small jar.

"Light up that candle," Grandma said, pointing to the candleholder on the table., "and bring it to me."

I conformed exactly. Then, Grandma had me stand near her. Holding the candle in front of her at chest level, she turned to her right, paused, and slowly lifted the candle saying, "To the Powers in the Rising Sun!" I turned and repeated what I just heard. "SHHHH! No need for you to call. Just watch." Grandma turned right again, paused, raised the candle, and said, "To the Powers of Midday!" But I wanted to do the ritual myself, not only to witness it. As I turned, I mentally repeated the words that I just heard; they resounded inside my head as powerfully as if I would have said them aloud. Grandma turned yet another quarter to the right, lifted the candle, and said, "To the Powers in the Setting Sun". Another turn: "To the Powers of Midnight". Last turn brought us both facing the direction where we had begun. Grandma looked up, and raised the candle high up over her head. I forgot that I'm supposed to just watch and found myself imitating her. It went unnoticed. Grandma's eyes were half-closed and in that moment, she seemed quite oblivious to my presence. "To the Powers in the Sky Above," she called, then bowed, lowered the candle, and said, "To the Powers in the Earth Below". She stood upright, her eyes –wide and glossy – gazed into nowhere. I wondered if she could still see me. She held the candle steady in front of herself and called one last time. "To the Powers that I…" Her voice, melodious and clear at first, faded to whispering, and then her lips barely moved without a sound coming out. Everything stood still. Then the candle began to flicker. A very light breeze swept through the space, and the floral fragrance that I recognized as the same from a few weeks before, floated around us. I first thought it may have something to do with the herbs that Grandma placed on top of the dresser. But no, I could smell fresh roses and there was no such thing in the room. I got goosebumps.

Finally, Grandma put the candleholder on the corner of the dresser, and asked me to open the small jar. I unscrewed the cap, and waited for her to pull a bit of dry herbs from the first bunch.

"What is this, and what is it good for," Grandma asked while holding a sprig in front of me.

"Basil," I answered without hesitation. "Good for chasing away anything bad, like bad spirits and demons."

"Very good. Now hold it in your palms. Close your eyes and ask Basil to lend its power to the blessing water that we make."

I held the basil sprig between my palms and spoke to the herb. My palms tingled. Or maybe it was just the spring of basil tickling my hands. Grandma asked me to put the herb in the jar and crumple it to fit close to the bottom. Then she took a sprig from the next bunch of herbs. As before, she asked me to identify it and name its uses.

"Sage," I said," good for keeping bad spirits away, like basil, but sage also makes one feel calmer and lighter, like sweeping the anger away. Oh, this is why you burned sage in my room the day before..."

"Yes," Grandma interrupted," and sage is also good to burn or sprinkle in the room of a sick person, whether they are physically, mentally, or emotionally unwell."

Guided by Grandmother, I held the sprig between my palms, and asked Sage to lend its powers to the blessing water that we were making. Then I put the sage in the jar, and folded it to stay at the bottom. Finally, Grandma took out the third herb which I identified immediately: lavender.

"What do we use it for," she asked.

"It smells nice and we put it in the wardrobe and closets to keep moths away," I said.

Grandma laughed shortly. "We don't care about moths right now. What are its healing and magical uses, do you know?"

I slowly shook my head 'no', feeling embarrassed. Lavender: who knew that the stuff used for keeping moths at bay is also good for healing magic?

"Pay attention, because I expect you to remember this; lavender is calming in the same way sage is. It dissolves the bad, heavy feeling that permeates a space where an argument took place or where something bad happened. It feels in a sense more refreshing than sage, and it also propitiates the presence of certain powers, which we'll talk about more another time"

Holding the piece of the dried plant between my palms, I asked Lavender to lend its powers to the blessing water that we were preparing, and then stuffed it to the bottom of the jar, on top of the other herbs.

From a drawer, Grandma took a chunk of black rock, and gave it to me.

"Do you know what this is," she asked.

I hesitated: "Granite?"

"Yes. How does it feel?"

"Heavy, cold, like something very sturdy, hard to move around."

"What would you use it for?"

"To make the water, or whatever I'm preparing, stronger, I guess?"

"No. Don't think about the water that you are making: think of what you do with the water, who is benefitting from it and how."

"The water is meant to bless and cleanse my room from anything nasty, like anger, sadness, fears, any bad spirits that may hang around. Right?"

"Right. But why?"

"Because I stay a lot in that room, and I sleep in there, and all that nasty stuff can cling onto me, right? Last time you sprinkled blessed water in my room, you told me that I will sleep better and feel lighter in the morning, which I did."

"So, the granite shall lend to this water something that you need: strength and stability. You can't live with your head in the clouds, unless you have your feet firmly planted into the ground. You want to be calm and patient, enduring like granite itself, and not be easily tossed and turned around by spirits, good or bad, or feelings, good or bad. Ask Granite to lend its qualities, so you can partake each time you use this water, my dear."

The chunk of rock felt alive in my hands. I talked to it politely, then placed it in the jar, on top of the herbs. Then, Grandmother had me hold the bottle she took out first.

"This is water from melting snow. It is the best for making cleansing potions, or blessing water, which is what we are making now. I don't know why this is so, but my grandmother always did it this way. It is what I learned, so it is what I am teaching you. Now ask the water to make everything it touches clean and beautiful as the fresh snow, then pour it over the herbs and the rock in the jar to fill it up."

I did exactly as Grandma said. I was getting dizzy, and wished we would finish sooner.

"Are you all right," asked Grandma.

I nodded, not wanting to say anything that could alarm her. I had heard many times that it wasn't good to interrupt rituals.

"Ok. Bring your hands over the jar."

I placed my hands over the jar, palms facing down. Grandma hovered her hands over mine.

"I call the Powers..." she completed the sentence mentally I believe by adding the names of those whom she so often called in.

I said in my mind: "I call those Powers that Grandma calls on, the Powers who helped me get well when I was sick, the Powers to whom I promised I'd be their friends then and always." I leaned my chest and belly against the side of the dresser, afraid that I may fall down.

"Sit down!" Grandma pointed to the armchair. "I will finish this by myself and give it to you."

"I'm fine!" I nearly shouted, and the sound of my own voice emboldened me. "We are finishing this together."

For whatever the reason, Grandma did not insist. Maybe she didn't want to bring in any anger that would arise from arguing with me, the very energy that she was seeking to cleanse within and around me. It was the whole purpose of the blessing water that we were preparing.

"When you do this by yourself, you don't have to call for any powers," said Grandma, not knowing that I had already made those calls albeit mentally. "It is enough for you now to ask Basil, Sage, Lavender, Granite, and the Snow Water itself to cleanse, purify, and render healthy and most pleasant anything this mixture touches, whether it is yourself, your belongings, or the space around you."

It took me some time to do what she said. I tried to concentrate and focus the energy as Grandma had just mentioned. When I was done, she asked me to put the lid on the jar.

"We are going to leave it by the window tonight. It is the last night of the Full Moon, and it is great to have the lunar power added to this preparation. In summer, we can leave it outside, on the balcony, but if we do so now, the water will freeze and break the jar. Let's end the ritual."

I didn't say anything, being barely able to stand. My eyes followed Grandma as she picked up the candleholder, raised it slightly, and thanked collectively to all the Powers that assisted us in the ritual. My nose caught the scent of roses again, and I felt like a gentle swirl passed by and caressed my cheeks. For one moment I forgot about feeling miserable. Then, Grandma left the candle on the dresser, and I watched her walking rather briskly around the room holding out her right arm.

"Grandma, I don't feel well," I finally admitted, and threw myself onto the armchair.

"Lay on the floor, and put your legs up the chair to let the blood reach the brain faster." The medical nurse replaced the granny. I did what she said and felt better almost immediately. In another couple of minutes, I jumped on my feet.

"Slowly! Sit down. Get another cookie. No, two. Here's water. Drink."

I did all that she said.

"I hope you understand that this is not a children's game, and in order to work with the bigger Powers, you must be a little bit older. You know now the full ritual of making blessing water. I did not explain all the details, how to prepare the space and call the Powers and the Guides, because as I said, you will have to wait until the time is right. However, you can prepare the blessing water simpler, by just calling on the spirts of the herbs, rocks, and the water that you use. Then, leave the jar in sunlight and moonlight. I wanted you to know how to prepare this all by yourself, to have it handy whenever you need. You can asperse your room, your bed before going to sleep, the clothes that you are about to wear, and yourself – just few drops on your forehead and your chest."

"Did you make the exact same water for Marius? I mean, did you use the same herbs and granite?"

"No. His needs are different. Also, Amelia asked me to use holy water that she brought from the church instead of snow water. The herbs that I used for him were basil, sage, and mugwort. In addition to the properties that you know about, these herbs also have another one in common: they can reverse curses. Yes, you heard me well. Don't look at me like that. What's done it's done, but it obviously needed some undoing. I used a white stone for him. I asked the Powers to give strength and determination to Marius, and make his bones strong as the rock itself."

I thought that was a lot to remember, and politely declining Grandma's invitation to play cards until dinnertime, I told her that I want to go to my room to think about what I learned. When I reached the door, I turned once more toward her:

"Thank you, Granny. I am so happy that I learned this from you. Can I also have my notebook back please? I wish to write everything down."

"No. Three quarters of what you wrote there is about cursing, binding, and banishing. You eavesdropped too much, and focused on the wrong things. Look, I will not deny that there is a place for darker and more aggressive magic. Think of it this way: if you go into the wilderness and some animal attacks you, you have to have a knife or a rifle to fend off the animal. But that is an extreme case, because you don't have to go into the wilderness to begin with. Don't look for trouble, so you don't need aggressive magic to keep you safe. Understood?"

I nodded, grinned, and left the room. I truly had plenty to think about.

I spent the next couple of hours writing down all that I got from Grandma that afternoon. Joyfully, I looked at the jar of blessing water sitting on the windowsill in my room. Then, when I put all the sheets of paper underneath the rug, I realized that the hideaway reached its maximum capacity. If I were to add any more, the noise of rustling paper would betray its presence when someone walked over it. Finding another safe place where to keep all my documented witchy work became a priority. I had to abandon the initial plan, to tuck a notebook behind the painting hanging in my room. I had found a way to actually do it, but any notebook that I tried to fit in there slipped out and dropped inadvertently whenever I'd close the door more forcefully, or chased the cat around.

After dinner, I began to pack my stuff for school for the next day. As I opened the schoolbag, I had an idea. By design, the boxy brown leather bag had a rectangular, rigid piece laid on the bottom to keep it laying flat: that piece was removable. A smaller size notebook, such as the one I was planning to use, fitted perfectly underneath. Unless someone stole my bag and took it apart, my witchy notes would have been safe there.

I went to bed with my head full of thoughts, most of them contradictory. At school and at home I heard repeatedly about the importance of being honest and always telling the truth, no matter how difficult that may be. But when I spoke my truth about what I believed in, who I believed to be, and what I cared about, not only did it get me into trouble but it seemed that it could have hurt my family as well. I had a gift, as Grandmother put it, and I was forbidden to talk about it because of the rules that governed the society we lived in. That was in stark conflict with being open and honest, the qualities that my teachers, my parents, and the society itself praised so highly. Up until about three months ago, I believed that sharing openly with other kids about the little wonders that spiced up my everyday life would gain me friends who then would also feel encouraged to share about the little wonders in their own lives. It always struck me as unfair that nobody ever spoke about anything similar to what I was speaking about. Despite feeling frustrated, I still believed that if I kept being honest and say more, other kids would eventually begin to reciprocate. Instead, I saw them pulling away. My classmates only flocked around me when we needed to form study groups, and dispersed quickly after the project or the assignment was over. Fortunately, the recent discussions with Grandma made me understand that not everyone could see what I saw, and among those who did even fewer would ever talk about it. By society's standards, I was either a weirdo, a psycho, or a pathological liar. Therefore, too much honesty in that regard was not going to get me anywhere.

But that didn't feel right at all. I did not want to be dishonest: I just wanted to be who I was, and be allowed to find my place among others. I thought then of artists, musicians, and writers who in their early lives kept their passions secret for fear of ridicule or other personal reasons. Sheltering a secret about themselves didn't necessarily make them dishonest. Similarly, I could simply keep my interest in esoteric things private, sheltered from anyone except my own grandmother. Then, I thought about how Grandmother herself was so careful and discreet about her own practice of folk healing and magic. Maybe there was no way to do it other than mainly solitary and wrapped in secrecy. I had read in Marius' history textbook about the persecution against witches during the eighteenth and nineteenth centuries. Ironically, the Church hunted witches, and years later, state authorities turned against the Church in several countries such as France after the French Revolution, and in radical Communist ones such as the Soviet Union. Having to surround my practice with discretion didn't feel so oppressive anymore. Putting things into a broader context, I felt lucky. In Romania, some things could still fly under the radar, such as the private preschool I had attended. Legally, that was not allowed. Practically, it ran underground and it did so quite well. Or taking Vica, for example: legally, no one was allowed to hire anyone else privately. According to the law, having a house maid was illegal. But technically speaking, Vica wasn't employed in our house. From a nearby village, Vica came to the city to complete her education. My family knew hers, and Vica was particularly fond of my mother. In exchange for housing and food, Vica offered to help around the house and keep an eye on me. She had less than one year until graduation from professional school, and my parents were glad to have her stay with us until she'd find employment and settle on her own. But it wasn't Vica's biography that I was interested in analyzing. I was concerned with discerning the fine line between honesty, privacy, discretion, avoidance, and blatant lies. Vica's connection, position, and relationship with our household was one such example of walking a fine line between playing by the rules, and breaking them. Gradually, Grandma's words acquired a deeper meaning: when dealing with oppressive regimes, lay low; don't give up or abandon whatever was important and valuable, but just don't draw attention to oneself. If that was the rule that applied to an entire nation, I could definitely scale it down to fit my own life. I sighed with relief, rolled over, and fell asleep.

Chapter 9

I had just come home from school. I was taking off my boots when the phone rang. Since I was sitting right next to it, I answered. Marius asked whether I was going to come over. Then his grandmother took the receiver from his hand and asked to speak with Grandma. Shortly after, Grandma and I headed to Marius' house. As soon as Mrs. Demeter opened the door, I could sense the electric atmosphere. Marius' grandmother and Mrs. Demeter threw themselves toward Grandma who disappeared in the collective hug. Marius was seated in the wheelchair. The two of us had never been huggly-snuggly toward one another, so we just shook hands and exchanged pats on the shoulders.

"Guess what," said Marius, before I could open my mouth, "today I stood up and walked two full steps. You are the best coach," he smirked, pulling me closer so no one else could hear, whispered, "and your grandma is better than all the doctors put together."

My eyes grew wide. Amused to see my face, Marius continued:

"I figured out that it has to be some folk medicine, some witchy thing, since my grandma sprinkled some stuff in my room and even washed my leg with it. So, it is true that your grandmother is that kind of medicine woman! Wow. Does she teach you any of this?"

"Well... uh, I kind of try to ..."

"Yeah, I got it. She's keeping it secret. I heard that this knowledge must be kept secret and only transmitted to the right person at the right time..."

"Wait, who told you these?"

"I heard my grandfather – this was a while ago – telling my grandma that she should, um... not be such close friends with your granny." Marius' cheeks flushed, and he looked to the side for a moment, visibly embarrassed. I pretended I hadn't noticed, and asked:

"But why?"

"My grandpa, you know that he was a priest before...well, grandpa has his own beliefs. He says that old folk medicine is not so good because healers can't really tell what's the source of their healing powers. He believes that only priests can heal properly through prayers and by saying the mass for the afflicted person. He had a friend of his saying a mass for me a while ago. Maybe you and your grandma helping was the answer to his prayer."

I nodded vigorously. I believed that could have been the case.

"Are your mom and grandma going to tell your grandpa about this other kind of healing that you received? Maybe this will convince him that there are good people doing healing who are not necessarily priests, like my grandma."

"Oh, no, absolutely not. Mom and grandma are going to keep it a secret, and told me to do the same. This is not something we can discuss with grandpa who is very stubborn when it comes to certain things, like the power of priests and the rules set up by the Church."

I rolled my eyes so far that I could probably see the insides of my head; then I burst into laughter. Marius began laughing without knowing why, which in turn made me crack up even harder. I barely managed to articulate: "It is....almost...the same...in our own...house."

Marius doubled down in his chair and I sat on the floor, both of us cracking up hysterically. We no longer knew whether our tears were caused by laughter or we were actually crying. All I could tell about Marius and me was that we were dumping off months of anxiety, grief, anger, and fear. And while our reasons were quite different, we both found so much healing in that uncontrolled, uncensored emotional outburst.

Marius' progress was unforeseeably quick. By the time the snow melted and the trees acquired tinges of green, Marius, supported by crutches, could go independently wherever he wanted. I had convinced him that going up the stairs, something that he understandably dreaded, was a great way to strengthen his legs. I was going less to his house, not because his recovery made him less interested in being friends with me, but because finally, Marius could walk over to our house. We could finally wander off into the woods, come back muddy, and drive our grandmothers nuts. A couple of friends that have been close to Marius all along, joined us. Hanging out with fifth graders made me feel important. For the past months, I had been around an incapacitated Marius, a person whom I discovered to be very, very different from the bully I had known. However, Marius was regaining his strength and his position as a leader among his peers. When that began to happen, I feared that I'd be cast aside. Marius could have felt embarrassed to be seen hanging around with a little kid. But that seemed not to be the case. The four of us, Marius, his two friends, and me, became almost inseparable. We usually gathered in the gazebo in our yard or on the porch at Marius' house, to eat, play cards or games, talk about the books that we read, or study for the approaching end of trimester exams.

Father was barely showing up at home, and when he came, he was tired most of the time. He had less time to talk to me than ever before. One day, I pulled out from under the bed the bow and quiver that he gave me for Christmas. The fact that he bought a bow instead of spending time with me to make one, casted a little shadow. Then, I felt anger surging because in the meantime, it became quite clear that my archery lessons and me joining an archery club would never happen. I didn't give into anger though. I breathed to calm down. I sat there for a while, patting my bow and looking absentmindedly at the treetops visible from my window. Next minute I was running down the stairs to the phone.

Since Marius loved the idea, the next day after school, the two of us, joined by his two best friends, were taking turns with my new, big-kid bow and arrows, teaching ourselves how to shoot on the improvised range, in the woods behind the house. Marius had the hardest time. If he held the crutches, he could not wield the bow, and letting go of the crutches scared him terribly. He was afraid of falling and re-injuring his leg. One of his friends came with the idea of finding something that Marius could sit on while shooting. We gave up quickly on that plan though.

"What if we support Marius as he stands up," his other friend suggested, and we all agreed.

Marius, still holding on to his crutches, positioned his legs first. Then his two friends and classmates kneeled and firmly grabbed his waist and hips. As Marius slowly let go of the crutches, I took them away. Then I handed him the bow and one arrow. It was hard to tell who among us was more nervous. The first arrow flew somewhere in the bushes nearby. I expected Marius to feel frustrated. He laughed instead and asked for another arrow.

"Here," I said, and helped him get the quiver on his back. "You shoot all six. I guess it's easier this way."

Three arrows later, one of the boys spoke.

"Marius, I believe that your legs are strong enough to support you, man. We were bracing you, using all our strength at first, but we are barely supporting you now. You are basically standing on your own. We just make sure that you don't lose balance and topple off which I don't think it's even likely to happen."

Marius didn't say anything. He shot the last two arrows, sweat dripping off his brow.

"I need to sit down, guys."

I took the bow, gave him the crutches, and then we all sat down on a log a little outside the range. Marius was both glowing and shaking nervously when he spoke again.

"I could feel my legs strong and steady. I have been so afraid that they can't take my body weight again..."

"What are you talking about, man? Your legs can hold you up just fine," spoke one of Marius' friends. "You were standing there shooting arrows five minutes ago. It's in your mind, dude, in your mind and nowhere else. Seriously."

Shortly after, we headed home. I was wondering how Marius' family would react upon hearing the account of all that happened.

The humming of the students reading their lessons made me want to go to sleep. I knew the bit of text almost by heart, and I had zero motivation to go over it again.

"Why isn't the teacher asking us questions already? How long does everyone need to read three short paragraphs and write the main idea of each? Third grade can be at times so boring!"

I began drawing bunnies at the end of the notebook to kill some time, and with it, my boredom. I thought of writing a poem, but since I had no idea of what exactly the poem should be about, I gave up. Then, finally, Mrs. Moisa's voice called for silence:

"Let's see, what is the main idea in the first paragraph?" The teacher's question broke both the monotonous humming and the painful boredom arising with it. A few hands shot up in the air, mine among those. I had eyes for nothing but the clock on the wall: only half an hour left until spring break.

When the bell rang, I slingshotted myself down the corridor and into the school yard. Middle-school kids, who began classes at 1:00pm, started to line up in front of the main entrance. I had time to quickly shake hands with Marius, who reminded me that he'd be home by 6:30pm.

"I'll drop by right after dinner," I said. "And I have a surprise from you."

"What is it?"

"If I'll tell you, then it's not a surprise anymore." I ran away, laughing at the thought that Marius, such a curious person, had to wait another six hours to find out what I was talking about.

That day, when we practiced archery on our improvised range, Marius found out that the only thing that prevented him from standing independently was his own fear and lack of trust in himself. In the aftermath of that event, Marius began to rely more on his legs and less on the crutches. As a result, in about one week he began to walk around using two canes, and then just one. Marius was finally convinced that he would walk as well as before the accident, but one thought still kept nagging him: how was he supposed to transition from walking to riding his bike again considering that he was highly risk-averse toward the perspective of falling. But I had an idea.

Marius didn't quite get the reason why I showed up at his door, carrying my scooter. He got even more confused when I handed it to him.

"What's this for," Marius asked.

"What was the first thing that you learned how to ride?"

"A tricycle," Marius answered, mildly surprised.

"Tough luck then, because we don't have any tricycle in your size. Anyway, I thought it may be a good idea to retrain your balance on a scooter, before getting back on the bike."

Marius shifted from surprised to perplexed.

"How come I never thought of it?"

I shrugged my shoulders, and seeing his hesitation, I added, "Are you taking it, or what?"

Finally, Marius took the scooter by the handle, and walked inside. I followed. The door to the first room on the left closed quickly; I wondered who had listened to our conversation. About fifteen minutes later we were in the alley, ready for

Marius to try on the scooter. His father came with us, then his mom and grandmother joined. Marius and I were not the only kids playing in the alley at that time, but we were certainly the noisiest. My parents came out too, and at some point, my family and Marius joined the conversation. They had never been exceedingly fond of each other, but over the past months I noticed that more casual and relaxed interaction replaced a certain rigidity. It must have been close to 9:00pm, when we all parted ways. "We have been invited to the Demeter's on Easter Sunday," Mother said. "What do you think?"

"I think I need new clothes," I said, pleasantly surprised about the turn of events.

"Don't touch it!" Grandma picked up the plate quickly. "This is not for you. It is a ritual offering."

"For who?"

"For fairies," Grandma said hesitatingly. "You know that the feast of Rusalii[8] is approaching, and in addition to that, this is the time of the year when offerings are made to those fairies who protect the household."

"I'll help," I said promptly. "I always wanted to make friends with fairies."

Grandma sighed, and I didn't understand why.

"Fine," she said. "After all, back in my day, this was a ritual where children could participate if they'd like. Wash your hands and face, put on a clean shirt at least, and then come here. I'll be waiting for you."

I flew out of the kitchen and up the stairs to my room. A ritual for fairies, oh my!! I washed my face and hands as Grandma asked me to, I let my hair down, brushed it carefully, and put on a blue headband. I picked up my favorite dress, teal-blue with white lace collar and cuffs. I put on the new shoes Mother bought for me to wear for Easter, raided my parents' bathroom and helped myself to Mother's perfume, and finally went back downstairs. Grandma gave me a look, as if she saw me for the first time.

"It's a ritual for fairies, right? They may come any moment, right?" I spoke with such excitement that I made Grandma laugh.

"You look like a princess."

Mother walked in, carrying groceries. Since Vica was away visiting her family during spring break, Mother and Grandma were the only ones in charge of the kitchen. Mother put down the bags and her eyes fell on me.

"Oh, where are you going dressed up like this?"

"Hi, Mom. Do you like it?" I turned around so she could see me from all angles.

"You look absolutely beautiful. But you haven't told me yet where you are going."

"I am helping Grandma make offerings to the home-protecting fairies. I dressed nice in their honor." As I finished my sentence, a cloud passed over Mother's face. I worried.

"I need to talk to you right now," Mother told Grandma, with visible irritation.

Grandma steadied herself in anticipation of what seemed to be an unavoidable argument. I didn't need anybody to tell me that Mother was unhappy about Grandma involving me in a fairy ritual.

"As I talk to your mom," said Grandma in a firm voice, "you take the plate with offerings outside, and put it on the table in the gazebo. Also, bring three clean glasses with fresh water. Pull three chairs near the table, and make sure the chairs are clean of dust. I'll bring the candle, and we will light it up together."

I did as I was told. After a while, Grandma came and brought a lantern with a candle inside. She took the candle out of the lantern, and asked me to light it up and then put it back inside. I sat the lantern at the center of the table, I pushed the plate a little closer and I placed the three glasses of water to correspond to the three chairs. Grandma looked around and nodded with contentment. She closed her eyes, and spoke aloud.

"We ask the Goodly Inclined Ones to come and enjoy our offerings. Kind ladies, bestow your blessings and protection over this household and those who live in it."

Silence dropped following Grandma's words. For a few moments nothing moved. Then, birds began to chirp, hens to craw, a dog barked somewhere, and from afar, floating on the wind, the mingling voices of people reached us. All that background noise was in such a stark contrast to the silence from only moments ago!

"Is this the way you learned from your own grandmother," I asked Grandma.

"Well, it wasn't exactly the same. First, my grandmother and my mom made a small fire of three special woods: hazel, maple, and dogwood. On the offering plate there were three braided buns, butter, and honey – the same as we have here now. There were three cups of water, and a larger water jug, for the visiting fairies to refresh themselves before eating. Three chairs were left around the fire, for them to sit and warm up after eating. We also used to burn myrrh and frankincense for them. Each child in the household used to participate in some way, no matter how small, in this ritual."

"Can we leave out water for them to wash, and burn some incense?"

"Would you like to do that?"

I nodded eagerly.

"Then you bring a dish of water, and I'll bring the censer."

Minutes later, a copper basin filled with water sat on a side table in the gazebo, and curls of smoke were rising from the censer. The sun was setting. The braided buns glowed golden in the candlelight.

Grandma took my hand, and we walked toward the house. I was excited but also a little disappointed.

"They didn't come, did they?"

"Maybe they did, maybe they didn't. Maybe they drew close to observe us, and will come later. You know, with very few exceptions, fairies do not want to be seen by people. And this is not something we should be talking about."

"Is Mother upset with you for allowing me to do the offerings?"

"I believe she's fine now. I explained to her that we cannot, and should not, lose everything we know, nor renounce everything we believe in. There are still many spiritual practices that can be done discreetly. Anything glamorous, too much in the open, anything related to spiritual healing, anything overtly magic could land us in jail. However, you see that there are some churches still open – more in the countryside than in the city – and as long as priests don't speak against the Party and don't mix into politics, they are relatively safe. You know what is interesting? Even some among the political leaders of the highest rank, deep down within themselves still do believe in God, albeit claiming the opposite. Leaders of organizations affirm they don't believe in anything supernatural in order to be in agreement with the political orientation, but when it comes to demolishing churches, few really feel comfortable signing a permit. If we are discrete, we are safe."

Bottom line, I thought, everyone had something to hide: witches had to hide their whereabouts from clergy and law enforcement, people in law enforcement and those holding various public offices had to hide their own beliefs from one another. I found the thought quite amusing. And I truly hoped mother understood Grandma's words. To me, they made perfect sense.

Things took a downturn early on Friday when Marius and I found ourselves promoted to the rank of Grandma's helpers in the kitchen. I protested mildly at first and tried to make up excuses, but to my dismay, Marius was quite happy to take the bowl off my hands and stir butter and sugar into cream.

"This requires strength," he said, filled with self-importance.

I settled for breaking egg shells, separating yolks from whites. For once in my life I missed Vica who went to spend the holiday with her family. But there were some perks to our new job: chocolate nibs, dried fruit, and nuts – Grandma made sure that we got generous portions of all goodies. Then, she assigned us to various little tasks, and left the kitchen. A few minutes later, we discovered the strawberry jelly...

When Grandma came back, one jar was empty. She got upset. We received a good scolding, not so much for having eaten a whole jar of strawberry preserve, but for our greediness which was likely to get us sick. Of course, Grandma was right. Shortly, both Marius and I were as nauseous as one can be, after having gobbled an enormous amount of jelly. Not only had Grandma no help in the kitchen at that point, but she was also left to care for two wretches plagued with pains and nausea.

I was too sick to even feel surprised or worried when Marius' grandmother walked in, probably upon Grandma calling her. Miss Amelia picked up the work right from where Marius and I had abandoned it. Mother came home from the hairdresser, and panicked when she saw us sick. Grandma, with her usual calm, restored order. While she helped the two of us settle outside on the back porch, Mother and Mrs. Amelia were directed to take over the kitchen. Marius stretched out on a lounge chair and I sat down on the floor, leaning against the wall. Grandma left us alone for a few moments. When she came back, she was carrying a large basin, towels, and a pitcher with water. From the apron's pockets, she pulled out the ceramic dish into which she burned things, matches, and a small bunch of something that looked like animal hair, tied with red thread.

She lit up the tiny bundle of hair, put it in the bowl, and circled Marius several times wafting smoke toward him. Then she came near me and did the same thing. Why did she burn something so horribly smelling? I voiced my question out loud.

"You ate like pigs; this is pig hair that I'm smoking you with. It will help your indigestion, one way or another."

She continued the "fumigation" as she called it. Then Grandma sat down near Marius, spat on her fingertips and began massaging his right forearm with upward movements running from his wrist toward the elbow. Between bouts of nausea and belly cramps, I could discern her murmuring:

"Go away aplecată[9]
You are unwanted,
You are cursed,
I am nagging you and pocking you,
and squeezing you out of this belly and out of this body
Out of these legs,
And out of these arms,
So Marius shall remain
Clean and fresh like flowers in the field,
Tall and vigorous like a fir tree."

After a while Marius began to yawn. Grandma finished rubbing his forearms and temples, spat three times over the top of his head, as if aiming at an invisible opponent standing behind Marius, and told him to get off the lounge chair and sit somewhere else. She explained that Marius sitting there where the healing charm was affected could undermine the cure. He came to sit next to me, visibly invigorated.

Grandma poured water from the pitcher into the small basin and rinsed her hands.

"Water, water coming," she shouted before dumping it out over the porch's rail.

Grandma's gesture did not surprise me since I was familiar with that practice, but it did surprise Marius.

"Mrs. Maria, why did you shout before dumping the water? There's nobody in the yard."

"And how can you be so sure there isn't somebody there? You must always shout out a warning before dumping out water, like this. If any zâne are passing, then it would be very rude to throw water on them, not to mention how dangerous this could be."

Marius listened without blinking nor breathing. As Grandma spoke, I saw his expression changing from incredulous to outright worried.

"Zâne, you mean fairies? Are they real? And do you have fairies coming into your yard?"

Grandma didn't answer. She walked down the porch and snapped a twig of basil from the closest bush. She poured again a little water in the basin, dipped the basil in, and aspersed the place where Marius had sat. Then, she asked me to lay in the lounge chair. I dragged myself over there. Grandma spat on her fingertips.

"Ew!" I interjected. "That's gross! Can't you use water please?"

My remark annoyed Grandma ever so slightly.

"Spittle has power. It is used in healing. It is used in cursing. So no, I am not using water."

I rolled my eyes and gazed somewhere else to overcome my disgust. It didn't make me wince when I saw spit used on Marius, but having it rubbed on myself...

"Can someone use holy water instead," asked Marius.

"You could. But what if there's no holy water at hand? And why not use spittle, as it had been done for many hundreds of years, before holy water was even a thing? Spit is sacred and powerful, I'm telling you."

None of us could argue against that. And who would dare to argue anyway against Grandma, the woman who with a little smoke and spittle could make the worst indigestion go away in a matter of minutes?

Easter Sunday came, bright and sunny, as my own disposition. I was aware of the religious meaning of the holiday. I had read a few iterations of the Biblical stories but I didn't like those too much. So, for me, celebrating Easter was centered on the arrival of the Easter Bunny. On behalf of the aforementioned rabbit, I always got new shoes and a new dress for Easter. There were also some customs that I loved. One was painting eggs. Another was washing the face on Easter morning with cold water in which a red-colored egg and a silver coin were placed; it was meant to bring beauty and good health to those observing that tradition. The best part though was visiting with friends. Whether we were the guests or had guests coming over, I had no recollection of any Easter Sunday devoid of merriment. For my family, Easter, same as Christmas, were cultural and social rather than religious events.

Grandma used to go to church sometimes, and occasionally I would go with her. I remember enjoying it thoroughly. The lighting of candles and praying near them, the heavy incense smoke, the old icons framed in silver and gold glittering in the dim light – it felt like a magic ritual, just on a bigger scale. I couldn't see much difference between spellwork and praying in church, and maybe that would explain my enjoyment.

I also remembered that last year, on a couple of occasions, the priest barely answered Grandma's greeting. Later, during mass, I heard the same priest speaking vehemently about the "demonic practices that many women still engage in." The allusion was obvious. On the way home I asked Grandma if she was upset about what the priest said.

"I used to be upset. That was many years ago. Then, I learned that people can be narrow-minded; and priests are also people. They say mass and walk inside the sanctum, but that alone doesn't make them different from the rest of us. They spent many years studying and reading about the lives of saints, the history of the church itself, how to say mass – they are very learned, and put their lives in service to the Church. But none of the priests that I know see anything outside what they were taught. Their knowledge resides in the books they read, and believe that facts of life are good or bad according to how those books label them. I feel good about what I do, and no priest is going to change my mind about this."

I accompanied Grandma to church that morning, while my parents stayed home. The priest aspersing holy water all around, using a bunch of dried basil made me think of Grandma's healing charm that she did the day before: she also dipped basil into water to "cleanse" the space around, especially the place where Marius and I laid while she worked on us. I couldn't help but wonder why the Church condemns so harshly the work of doftoroaie or witches when they do so much of the same thing. Now, to overly generalize and say that all witches that I knew were all candid beings who never wished ill to anyone, was a stretch. My own Aunt Camilia was living proof, and I had to look no farther than any mirror at hand to get a good look of someone who didn't think twice before seeking revenge through cursing. Sorting out good and bad wasn't that easy, so I decided to focus on the day ahead and the promises of fun and merriment that it held in store.

Chapter 10

Hopping and skipping, I arrived home, eager to tell my parents that the big competition was exactly two weeks away. I had a letter from my teacher asking one of my parents to accompany me to the city library and help me check out a couple of books not available in the children's section. Grandma was sitting with Mrs. Amelia. My enthusiasm dampened a little when I found out that my parents were out, because it meant that I would not make it to the public library right away as I thought I would.

I changed from my school uniform to a dress and leggings. I was heading to the door when Grandma stopped me, insisting that I put on a jacket. While I had rolled my eyes at first, I soon came to thank her because, albeit early May, it was a chilly afternoon. I walked toward the woods. I passed the picnic table and benches at the bottom of our yard, and just stepped underneath the greening canopy.

"Hi! Do you want to play?"

I stopped abruptly and turned around. A girl about my age sat at the table I had just passed. I would have sworn that there was no one sitting there a moment ago. She stood up and ran past me, and into the woods, giggling. I ran after her. I ran as fast as I could, trying in vain to close the gap between us. I noticed that the girl wore a dress similar to mine, but sleeveless, as if she was impervious to temperature.

"Hey, slow down," I shouted, concerned that we were going way too deep into the woods.

She looked over her shoulder, and without slowing down, shouted back.

"Oh, you are safe as long as I am around."

That was uncanny. I felt shivers and my skin crawling. I stopped, panting. I looked around: not recognizing the surroundings was unnerving. I was torn between wanting to follow the girl and make friends, and the gut feeling telling me that I should find my way back home as quickly as possible. The girl had disappeared. No footsteps, no giggling, no noise whatsoever, nothing moved, not even a leaf. The air felt strangely solid and the trees stiff as if they weren't even real trees but some sort of stage décor. I looked quickly around to get an idea where the sun was setting. That was easy. I then realized that we ran west, following an approximately straight line. So, I only needed to turn on my heels and follow the same straight line, just in the opposite direction. I began trotting back, and shortly after, I was sitting at the dinner table with the whole family.

I didn't say a word about the strange encounter that I just had, directing instead everyone's attention toward the upcoming competition and the need I had for one of my parents to accompany me to the library. Mother volunteered to pick me up from school the next day and take me to the city library. Then, I followed Grandma up the stairs.

"Grandma, I must tell you something," I whispered.

"Don't you have any homework to finish for tomorrow?"

"I do, but this is urgent. I'm sure you want to hear about the girl that I just met."

"A new friend?"

"Well, I don't really know."

We entered Grandma's room, and as soon as we sat down, I told her about the uncanny encounter.

At first Grandma's eyes widened, then she gasped and covered her mouth with her hand.

"We shall ward your room first, then you can go about your homework."

"Ward?" I was surprised.

"Yes. They may try to reach you when you are alone in your room, especially during sleep."

"They? There was only one girl, and I am really curious about who she is and if we can be friends. I would have followed her if she'd only slowed down and acted less strange…"

"Shhhh. Listen here. The girl that you saw it's not really a girl…"

"It occurred to me that she may be some sort of spirit," I interrupted, "and this is why I wanted to talk only to you and no one else about the encounter." In the comfort of our house and in the ever-reassuring presence of my own grandmother, the unsettling feeling from earlier while I was in the woods vanished. Instead, I felt excited and brave enough to claim that I would be glad to see the girl again and talk to her.

"You are lucky that you didn't follow her any farther. We might have never seen you again. Come here and help me."

Grandma opened the drawers and doors to the chest where she kept everything she needed for her work. She gave me three bunches of dried herbs wrapped in brown paper, and a jar whose contents I recognized to be a mix of myrrh and frankincense. She picked up a few more things and motioned in the direction of the door. I led the way to my room.

I tossed and turned in bed, unable to go to sleep. The bed itself felt extremely uncomfortable, all bumpy and radiating heat. I threw away the covers, but the room was too chilly. I lifted the pillow and found the bunch of herbs Grandma placed there. She had said that those would make me sleep better and guard me throughout the night "against any less-than-benevolent spirits," as she phrased it. I picked the herbs up and inhaled their aroma with gusto. It felt soothing: mugwort[10], valerian[11], lovage[12], hyssop[13], and vervain[14], as Grandma named them for me as she tied them together with red thread. I put the herbs back under the pillow. I reached toward the nightstand, opened the drawer and took out my wand. I held it close to my chest: for others it was probably nothing but a twig with few maladroit carvings that betrayed the artist's age. But for me, that was my wand, the badge of office for the witch I deemed myself to be. Upon returning the wand, Grandma also gave me some ideas on how to use it to ward my room before going to bed and anytime I'd sense I needed warding. Grandma herself did not use wands, but seeing how attached I was to the image of wand-wielding witches and fairies, tried to come up with practical ways for me to use it instead of just having a wand as a mere piece of décor.

I got out of bed, and searched for my schoolbag. Something moved near the desk. I jumped back, my outstretched arm pointing the wand in the direction of the sound. I was just about to utter the banishing charm.

"Mrrr! Meow!" Two green dots shone from underneath the desk. I sighed with immense relief, lowered the wand, and explained to the cat that I was just about to curse him. I reached the bag still warm as the fluffy little feline left it, and put the wand together with my notebook. I smiled contently. One second later…

"Felix, no, no, no! You will get hurt!" I dived on my belly and slid under the bed to pull out the cat who found nothing better to do than play with the knife that Grandma put there.

"Silly cat!" I separated the two incompatible entities, the cat and the knife, dropped the first on the bed, and after a little bit of thinking, I put the second one inside my desk's main drawer. No matter how smart Felix was, he would not get the knife from there.

I tucked myself under the covers. The bed felt soft and welcoming as it had always been – the discomfort that I felt before totally gone. Could Felix' presence be so soothing? Could removing the knife make such a difference? Things just didn't add up in my head. The knife itself was placed under my bed as a protection against …whoever Grandma wanted to protect me against, so it should not have bothered me. Whatever. Purrr – the last thing my mind registered before checking out.

Chapter 11

I couldn't settle. I couldn't sit down. Any attempt at homework was frustrating as much as it was futile. The two books I got from the library, enthroned at the center of my desk, lay still untouched. Hearing that I am barely in third grade, the librarian gave me a month and a half to return them. I didn't have a month and a half at my disposal. When I told the librarian that I had to go through those books in two weeks she made a face... Anyway, I could probably focus on reading those to prepare for the competition, and ask the teacher for an extension on my other assignments. I got off the chair and began to pace the room, trying to organize the whirlwind in my head. Grandma skilfully avoided, so far, all of my questions about the Powers that she oftentimes mentioned generically and collectively, but never named individually. Also, I had every reason to believe there was so much more to what she was doing than she was actually sharing with me. Grandma had told me on different occasions that I should focus on practicing what I already knew, arguing that she had taught me plenty. Plenty? By whose standards? She had only taught me, I mean explicitly, how to clean and ward my space, and make blessed water. There was quite a bit more that I had "stolen" and the little spells of my own making, but those didn't count toward our bargain: Grandma had promised she would train me to be just like herself – whatever the exact meaning of that was – and I was going to keep her true to her promise, whatever it would take.

"For how long shall I still wait?" I kept asking whenever I saw the opportunity, and hoped that she'd succumb to consistent pestering.

"Until the time's right," she kept saying as consistent and predictable in her wording, as night following day. I would have ignored her annoying, stereotypical answer. But, over the past couple of weeks, I noticed a change. Grandma's tone conveyed vaguely, yet impossible to miss, that something was actually looming in the air. It made me mildly anxious. What kind of danger was lurking in the shadows, and what did it have to do with me wanting to learn all that she knew?

As soon as I got wind of a new gathering at Grandma's, I began pressing to gain access. The refusals, mild at first, gradually built-in intensity until they took the form of an irritated "NO!" – at which point I decided to try something else. I quickly turned to the "Observatory" but, to my frustration, I found the door locked: someone was using that space according to the purpose it was originally built for.

My first reaction was to get angry, but I quickly realized how lucky I had been to use the bathroom/observatory for as long as I did, without anyone "sitting" in my way (pun fully intended). I went quickly upstairs. Upon finding Vica by Grandma's door, impersonating Cerberus, I took a sharp left, and disappeared into my room. When would Vica finally leave our house? When would she finish school, find a job, get married, or whatever would take to make her leave? I thought about Mother, even Grandma, how fond they were of her, and rolled my eyes.

I so wished to do a spell to 'help' the situation! I hesitated at first, but after a brief negotiation with my own conscience, I decided to do something which I hoped would make Vica leave sooner rather than later. I got my notebook out from its hiding place inside the schoolbag. I began leafing through the pages, and was surprised to see how much content I had gathered. There were the procedures for warding the room and making blessed water, notes about herbs and their uses, the healing charm for indigestion, the charm for cough. There were also notes about stuff used for cursing, everything I could still remember from among the far richer material of that sort collected in the notebook that Grandma didn't want to give me back.

"Meow!"

"Hi Felix, do you want to help?"

The cat sat down and looked at me as if he understood what I said. I giggled.

"Ok, let's see what we need," I continued. "Dried red ants... where am I going to find red ants, and how am I supposed to dry them? Oh, here's the next ingredient: dry wasps. You know Felix, I can find that: I have an idea. Let's see what else do I need. Red hot peppers, dried and powdered: no problem. Brimstone – well, we don't have that. And then there's the move with the broom, and picking up dust from Vica's footprint. The broom is easy. To be right behind her and pick up dust from her fresh footprint, this may be more difficult. These are three different spells, but do you know something kitty? I'll combine them. Yep."

Talking to the cat helped me put things in perspective regardless of the fact that the audience had fallen asleep. I closed the notebook, and thought that it needed a name, something that was both defining and dignifying, something that would actually reflect the value of the treasured material it contained. Careful not to wake Felix, asleep on my lap, I opened the desk's drawer and after a brief moment of indecisiveness I picked up the black pen. About one minute later, the notebook's front cover read *Daniela's Little Book of Magic* neatly written in capitals. I admired my work while waiting for the ink to dry. I scratched Felix's head.

"What do you think of this, kitty? Grand, isn't it?" But Felix didn't share my enthusiasm: he stretched, jumped down, then climbed on bed where he continued his nap.

I had gathered all the spell ingredients and supplies on the windowsill. Had somebody walked into the room, they would only see my back, if that, since the drapery nearly touching the floor, covered me entirely. I opened the jar. Four dead wasps lay inside, the victims of the insecticide Vica herself had sprayed around the kitchen window the day before. I smiled at the irony. I dumped them in the garlic-smelling, wooden mortar I had "borrowed" from the kitchen. I took out of my pocket a red-hot pepper, broke it into tiny bits, and put it on top of the wasps. I made a mental note not to touch my eyes, nor pet the cat. I began grinding slowly. I could not remember the words exactly as I had heard them from Aunt Camilia when she had sent her ex-boyfriend packing, but I did take notes ample enough to be able to recreate the spell using my own wording.

"You'll go away, Vica, fast, as fast as you can, as if chased by furious, venomous wasps. You can't stay in this place anymore because your feet are burning like fire, like rubbed with hot red pepper. You will have no rest until you leave this house."

I repeated the incantation for as long as I ground the ingredients as finely as I could.

"And this is so," I said out loud, the words dropping strong and heavy along the mortar pounding one last time. What a sense of satisfaction! I collected the powder carefully in a paper envelope which then I folded and put into my pocket. A few minutes later I was in Vica's room spreading the get-the-heck-out-of-here mix on the carpet where she would surely walk through. Content with the outcome, I headed to the kitchen. I found Grandma alone, which meant that Vica was still at school. I asked Grandma if I could help.

"Is everything alright," Grandma asked, given that my request was a little unusual. I nodded emphatically, and explained that I needed a break from my school assignments. Grandma was happy to have me around, especially that I was not pestering with questions about any of the things that she did not want to talk about. We finished preparing dinner, left all pots and pans sitting on the stove, and sat down at the kitchen table.

"When I was about your age..." That was how the best stories always began. Without featuring any Cyclops, gods, or mythical heroes accomplishing impossible tasks, Grandma's stories outranked all the others. They were true stories, scary but also funny, and what rendered them really special was their protagonist, who was no other than the narrator herself. To spice things up, magic was always present, in bigger or smaller ways. I leaned back. Behind my closed eyelids, Grandma's words painted people and places, a world that seemed so far away yet so immediately near. All else went into oblivion.

I didn't even hear the backdoor opening, so Vica's apparition in the kitchen startled me. I opened my eyes, and took a few moments to reorient myself. Shortly after we gathered around the table for dinner. I enjoyed being the center of attention, receiving praise for my involvement in dinner preparation. Usually, I would have been the first one to go upstairs once the meal was over, but I found all kinds of excuses to stay behind. I went as far as volunteering to help Vica wash the dishes, which made everyone's jaw drop. I was waiting patiently for my nemesis to leave the kitchen, even briefly, so I could do the sweeping charm. Finally, Vica walked out the door, and headed toward the restroom. I grabbed the broom that I had brought out from the closet a short while ago. Long, slow strokes, imagining that I swept Vica herself out the door...and I stopped. Something was not right. That wasn't the right way to do it. I realized that I should wait for Vica to actually leave the house, go out, run some errand, or go to school. Disappointment must have been so evident, that Mother, who just walked in the kitchen, asked me if I was feeling well. I muttered something about the competition that was taking place the next day, and the fact that I was a little nervous.

"Would you like to review together one last time, before bedtime?"

I gladly took Mother's offer. Ever since the visit to the psychologist, she made visible efforts to connect with me. More often than not, she'd go out her way to meet me on my turf rather than trying to yank me out and pull me over to her side. I felt treated less like a little brainless doll and more as a person with feelings, thoughts, preferences, and a will of my own.

A couple of hours later, I turned off the light and slipped under the covers. Quite content with my level of preparedness, I was ready to go to sleep. There was a light knock at the door, then Grandma walked in. She sat down on the bed, and in the semi-darkness I could feel, albeit not seeing, her smile.

"I'm so proud of you," she said. "So little you are, yet bold, and talented in…so many ways. Which book was the most difficult to read, I mean, in preparation for tomorrow?"

"There's a stack on my desk. The book on top was the most challenging to go through."

Grandma walked to the desk, picked up the book, and came back to sit next to me.

"Listen here," she said, her voice lowered to whisper. "This is a little charm that I want you to remember. You are going to study a lot in your life as I can tell. There'll be a lot to remember, to memorize. This will help."

I sat upright.

"Take the book and put it under your pillow together with this." Along with those last words, Grandma tucked into my hand something wrapped in a paper napkin. Then she continued: "There's a bit of bread inside the napkin, which you are going to eat first thing upon waking up in the morning. As you eat the bread, say: "As this bread I eat does not part with my body, so the knowledge in the book shall not part with my mind." You will remember absolutely everything that you read."

Under grandma's watchful eye, I put the book and the bread under the pillow. She kissed my forehead, and tucked me in bed.

"Good night princess. You'll do great tomorrow, I'm sure."

The last bit of my worries vanished. I was sure Grandma could feel me smiling.

Chapter 12

"One more month of school," said Marius. The heat of the day kept us under the green, thick grapevine canopy stretching over the back patio.

The sudden wave of heat made us abandon our initial plans for the afternoon. The excitement about riding our bikes all the way down to the Danube River, only about four miles away, melted like an ice cube on the hot pavement. I looked at the bikes parked in the shade: what were we thinking?

"Shall we go shoot some arrows? It's cooler under the trees," I suggested, because truth being said, the heat bothered me far less than inactivity.

Marius gave me an imploring look.

"Ok, we are not going anywhere," I retracted, "and homework is done, so, let's play something." I probably sounded a little irritated, because as I said, there were very few things that I found more irritating than inactivity.

"Do you always have to do something? Do you ever just chill," asked Marius.

"No. I chill when I think, which is when I make plans about what I will do next."

The pause acquired material density. I felt the silence weighing on us, as if something momentous had ended its incubation and was just about to hatch. Marius broke the silence.

"I meant to ask you, what do you think about angels?" He tried to sound casual without too much success.

"About what?" I wanted to make sure I heard him correctly. Never before did Marius ask me directly about my own beliefs in the existence of anything that belonged to the supernatural realm. My face must have shown confusion which Marius misunderstood:

"Angels; and please don't laugh. I never laugh when you mention fairies…"

"No, wait, I am not laughing, and I was not going to make fun, I…."

We kept cutting each other off, blurting out half-formed thoughts. Marius was clearly concerned that I'd make fun of him. I wanted to reassure him that I wasn't, since I had my own less – than-ordinary experiences and many still unanswered questions. Yet, I was weary of giving too many explanations, concerned that I would let slip something that I shouldn't. I had promised Grandma that I would not talk about fairies or magic with anyone other than herself, and I really wanted to stay true to my word.

Marius misunderstood my hesitation.

"So, you don't believe in angels. I find it interesting, because your grandmother does all this amazing work and she probably calls on angels and saints. If you trust what she does, how come you don't believe in these beings?"

"Who told you what I believe and what I don't believe in? As a matter of fact, I believe that angels exist. Grandma knows stories about angels. There are icons and statues of angels and saints in church. I don't go to church too often, but when I do, I see people praying to them, and I heard of so many prayers being answered. So, of course, they exist, if you ask me."

There was a pause.

"Daniela, I saw an angel."

"Wow, cool. What did it look like?

I didn't sound surprised enough probably, because Marius said nothing but sighed, suddenly absorbed by the glass of lemonade in his hands. Silence followed. Marius chewed mechanically on the straw in his glass, his mind evidently absent. The sunlight turned the water droplets on the pitcher and glasses into liquid diamonds. While my eyes couldn't move away from the glittering, my mind couldn't focus on anything other than the question: how much could I trust Marius to tell him about the things that I could see?

Without taking his eyes off the glass of lemonade, Marius told me his story. While struggling through his painful recovery, he woke up one night to the feeling that he wasn't alone in the room. Not far from his bed he noticed a humanoid form, glowing softly. If not for the glow, Marius who was anything but fearful, would have explained the presence as some ordinary shadow caused by who knows what object in the room. Then, he would have rolled over and gone back to sleep. But the silhouette and the silvery glow surrounding it drew a little closer. Marius' first impulse was to scream, but his voice failed him.

"Yet almost immediately I felt this incredible peace and a sense of ease taking over me. Then, I somehow knew that everything would be alright and I felt both incredulous and hopeful – if it makes any sense. The angel disappeared, and I called for it to come back, whispering at first then out loud. I wanted so much to see that light again and feel the peace that it brought! I must have shouted because both my parents rushed into my room. I told them what happened, and mom checked to see if I ran a fever, which, of course, I wasn't. Grandpa sprinkled holy water and burned myrrh and frankincense in my room. He said that it could not be an angel, because only holy men and women, like monks and nuns, could see them. According to Grandpa, I was either hallucinating, or some other kind of being came over. Either way, for several days afterwards, he read prayers in my room and sprinkled holy water – to prevent it from coming back, I'd guess. But I really, really believe it was an angel."

Marius put so much passion in those words, and it was maybe the fervent tone that inspired trust and made me confide in him.

"Marius, I believe you. I totally trust that you were neither imagining nor dreaming. But why an angel and not something someone else, like a…fairy, for example?" I tried to sound light and casual when I mentioned the fairy.

Steeped as we were in our conversation, none of us heard Marius' grandfather walking on the patio.

"Hello, how are you doing? Too hot to run around?"

Old Mr. Demeter's booming voice startled us. I was so glad that I had not had the chance to mention anything more about my own interest in fairies. I wondered how much he overheard. I got my answer right away.

"Fairies, huh?" Marius Grandpa pulled a chair and sat down next to us. His black beard, tall stature, and slightly crooked back made him look intimidating. I never felt at ease around old Mr. Demeter.

"Fairies are not to be messed with. They are still around, and they will still be for as long as the world will last, until The Day of Judgment. Fairies are reminiscent of pagan times and are therefore demonic beings. The Church should not permit fairy-related customs. Good that Călusari[15] are excluded from the Holy Communion for three years after they dance in their annual ritual, although exclusion from Communion alone doesn't seem to deter anybody from participating. As soon as Easter is over, men flock around the elders, who should know better, if you ask me – to learn the darn performance, and then enact it during the week of Pentecost. The holiday should be all about the Holy Spirit, not about Rusalii."

Marius' Grandfather was working himself up into a fit of anger. "I don't care about what you read in your books about fairies. Those are junk. Children's stories should mention angels, not demonic beings, except to warn against them. You two listen here: you stay away from fairies and the like. You only pray to the One God, and to Jesus, his son. That's it. Understood?"

"Yes, sir," we answered in unison, exchanging distressed looks.

Rescue arrived in the person of Marius' grandmother.

"Children, if you have finished the lemonade, bring the glasses inside and wash them, please. Also, could you go buy a tub of ice-cream? I can't believe it's not even near the end of May. It hasn't rained in weeks and it is scorching hot..."

Old Mr. Demeter jumped at the opportunity:

"The Holy Scripture says that there will be seven years of drought to signal the approaching of Judgment Day..."

"Save preaching for church, dear, and let these children be. You'll give them nightmares."

Minutes later, we were pedaling as fast as we could, glad to have escaped the heavy discourse Marius' grandfather felt compelled to give us.

We took a detour through the park, the same park where Marius tried to get to on the day he got hit by the car. We rode on the main alley, around patches of grass, and around colorful flowerbeds. Once or twice, we timed our gimmicks badly and ended up soaked by sprinklers. I had a hard time keeping up with Marius who had been exercising almost obsessively. He was getting muscular and bulky, and I was glad I found myself on his good side because if it were to come down to fist-fighting I wouldn't have had the slightest chance.

"Who knew that physical therapy would turn you into an exercise addict?" I yelled out loud, trying to jump the bike up the curb, same as Marius. The following second I flew over the handle bar, crashed onto the pavement, and rolled into the flowerbed on my right.

"You ok? Have you ever jumped up on this one?" Marius came running, while I pulled my sore self up to a standing position. I shook my head, and began to brush mulch, soil, and purple pansies off my clothes. Marius went to check on my bike. The chain was out.

"No problem," he said. "We can put it back, it is not a big deal. Then I'll show you how to hop up that curb; it's the highest in the park, and it's also the trickiest. I didn't know you can't do it, otherwise we would not have come this way."

Marius took out a couple of keys from the toolkit he carried in the small pouch attached to the saddle, flipped my bike upside down, and in less than ten minutes the chain was back in its place. I had fallen pretty badly having hit the ground with my right hand, left elbow, and my forehead. I washed the scrapes and the cut on my brow with water from a sprinkler, and pressed hard with the handkerchief to stop the bleeding. Then, I rode around a little bit to get a feel for the bike and get over the dizziness. I reluctantly agreed to Marius' impetus to teach me the new bike trick; I would have done anything else but approach the jump again, yet I felt terribly embarrassed to admit that I was scared. He reassured me that it was actually easier than it looked, if done the right way. It was the "right way" in his sentence that worried me a little.

First, we walked and studied the terrain. Marius asked me to observe the slight slope that helped anyone riding downhill increase speed, and the angle at which I had to attack the jump. I understood immediately why I couldn't get enough height and why the front wheel hit the rim of the curb instead of flying over it. I told Marius what I thought.

"Of course, this is why you crashed. You can't come straight at it, like, you know, perpendicularly. Not with these bikes that we have. Watch me first. Then, go a few yards farther back, and follow my guidance exactly"

I watched Marius mounting his bike, then going down toward the black granite that hemmed the sidewalk. He came down at a slant, attacked the jump when about a foot away from the edge, and flew way above it. He made it look so easy! I took a deep breath, mounted, and started downhill accelerating as I drew near, following Marius instructions to the letter.

"NOW!"

I attacked without thinking, and held my breath. I landed a bit uncertain, nearly falling again.

"Wow, this feels amazing. I never jumped so high or so far." I could hardly contain my excitement. I burst into laughter, forgetting about my sore palm and the burning forehead.

"What took you so long?" Both grandmothers', mine and Marius', were waiting for us on the patio. I gave a shortened version of what happened, only mentioning that I fell off the bike and glorifying Marius salutary intervention. I didn't say a word about his ability as an acrobatic bike-riding coach.

"Then you really deserve some ice cream," said Marius' grandmother, handing each of us a cup and a spoon.

Marius motioned me discreetly toward the backyard. We left the ladies on the patio to continue their talk, and we walked up to the old bench beneath the linden tree. Linden flowers had just begun to open and their sweet fragrance filled the late afternoon.

"I don't care what Grandpa says; I am convinced it was an angel," Marius spoke between spoonfuls of ice cream.

"Why an angel, and not a fairy?"

"You said yourself that people go to church and pray to saints and angels for all kinds of things, and many then say they got their prayers answered. Right?"

I nodded.

"I had been praying for days to heal. So many times I had overheard my parents' worried whispered conversations about the lack of progress, that I gave into fear that I wouldn't walk again. My grandparents encouraged me to pray though, and I did just that – I prayed, oftentimes without one specific being in mind to whom I directed my prayer: God, saints, angels, I asked them all for help." Marius paused, visibly moved by his own emotions.

"So?"

"So, one night that being came over, and the next day you showed up, saying you had an idea about helping me. I'm sure an angel sent you…"

"Or a fairy," I interrupted. "Listen, I do believe angels exist and can appear to people. I heard from Grandma stories about angels, but I heard even more stories about men and women who do healing work with help from fairies. I believe Grandma knows a lot more about this but won't tell me. She also calls on Powers, but she never told me who those powers are. There may be angels among them, but also fairies. I don't know why; I really lean toward fairies."

"Why?"

"Why not?"

"Because angels are more friendly, and clearly on God's side. Didn't you hear Grandpa?"

"I don't know. I don't think your Grandpa is one hundred percent right. I don't believe all fairies are bad. I don't believe that all the stories that I heard about good things coming from fairies are made up."

"Then you also shall believe that not all stories about bad things done to people by fairies are made up either."

Marius had a point. My mind was teeter-tottering: good fairy, bad fairy, good fairy…

A bee landed on my hand, attracted by the ice cream. Marius recoiled.

"Oh gosh, it's a bee!" His pitch and tone made it sound like a fire-breathing dragon came about eying my hand as a potential snack.

"Sit still and keep quiet," I told Marius. "Hey, little bee, I'm ok with you crawling on my hand. Eat whatever you want. And thanks for the honey that you give us." The thread-like feet tickled my hand for another moment or two. Then, with a buzzzz, the bee took off. That gave me an idea.

110

"You know, I believe that dealing with fairies is a little bit like dealing with bees. We may get stung, sometimes without a reason, I mean without a reason that we can fully understand. We don't know how bees think. And I believe we don't know exactly how fairies think either. Things can turn out good or bad, but we ought to be nice if we want to get a better chance of good things happening."

"How can you be so sure you understand fairies?"

I took a deep breath.

"Umm, I don't, but I believe I encountered a fairy." I went ahead telling Marius about the encounter I had with the strangely-acting girl. The cat was out of the bag.

"Why do you think that was a fairy and not an angel," Marius asked. "She told you that you would be safe with her. Don't you know that children have guardian angels? Maybe that was yours."

"Maybe. But Grandma seemed worried. Angel or fairy, Grandma didn't seem ok with any being asking me to follow them deep into the woods at sunset. I haven't heard of mischievous angels, but I heard of mischievous fairies – so if this one was after mischief, then it's a fairy and not an angel. On the other hand, I liked her and I hope she comes around again. I kind of miss her, although I only saw her once. "

Both grandmothers came to get us home for dinner. While we could not agree whether we were seeing angels or fairies, Marius and I trusted each other's experience and vowed to never say a word to anyone else. Complicity felt good.

Chapter 13

As soon as Vica left home, I grabbed the broom and swept behind her, with the clear intent of her finding another place to go. Seeing her all dolled-up and smiling unctuously while in conversation with Mother, made me resent her even more. I could not forget her intervention on the day my books were one step away from being trashed. I believed Vica kept an eye on me hoping she'd catch me red-handed and turn me in to Mother or Father thus proving how reliable and loyal she was.

Without Vica at my heels, I had no problem going into Grandma's room when no one was inside. After briefly considering the situation, I hid under the round table where the ladies would shortly gather for coffee and psychic work. The burgundy velvet tablecloth with short and thick silk tassels touching the ground covered me perfectly. Under the table and hidden from sight, two slats of wood formed a cross that connected the four massive legs. Perched at the intersection of the slats, I curled into the tiniest pretzel my body could assume to occupy as little space as possible. I only had to pay attention not to betray my presence.

I had seen countless times my aunt reading cards, but only very few times did I hear her sound so agitated.

"Men of power will come into this house. It can turn out really bad."

"Could it be related to army drafting?' Mrs. Constanza asked tentatively. "With the Russians right at the border, one can never tell what tomorrow holds in store."

"No, I believe it's rather an uprising against the current government, who is the Russians' puppet. The stronger this Communism thing with the crazy ideas of collectivization and restriction to personal property goes, the less people can stand it." Mrs. Ileana spoke in an all-knowing tone.

"We shouldn't even be having this conversation. It's scary just to think of all these." What? Marius' grandmother was also part of the circle? If her husband, Marius' grandfather, knew about it... I could not even imagine what he would say or do.

"No. It is none of these," I heard my aunt's voice accompanied by her finger tapping hard onto a card. "Here. Look. Police will get here within a matter of days. It may turn either very bad, or the situation could clear completely. The resolution, good or bad, hinges on a young woman's words."

I could only imagine the worried looks on their faces. Aunt Camelia spoke again:

"Mother, could you please focus on the situation we face and ask about the solution? Your power is greater than any of us, and if anyone could retrieve that piece of information, that is you."

I heard Grandma sighing. Shortly after, I heard the crystalline sound of the porcelain cup meeting the saucer. So, Grandma concentrated on the query while sipping the coffee and Aunt Camelia would read the cup. No one was saying anything. I was so afraid to betray my presence that I barely breathed. My ankle began to itch and the more I tried to ignore it, the worse it got. There was movement around the table, and I caught the opportunity to scratch as silently as I could. My aunt began to read Grandma's coffee cup.

"Here. Military men are coming into this house. One of them is tall and wears a mustache. Oh, a very handsome man indeed." Of course, I thought, what could Aunt Camelia think of, other than handsome men? Her next words fell like pebbles on the still surface of a lake: from my hiding place I could feel the ripples. "There is a man, his name begins with C. Can't tell whether it is a first or last name. He faces a young woman, much shorter than him. This conversation they'll have can unblock the situation, like opening the way, or end very, very ugly. Look over here, can you all see this? The woman, certainly a young person, stands on a teeter-totter. No wait: she stands on a scale. Depending on what she does, the scale will tip one way or the other." I was ready to bet that no one could see anything in that cup, no matter how much she'd point out; each time Aunt Camelia tried to teach me how to read coffee grounds, all I could see was, well, coffee grounds. However, nobody ever dared to voice the slightest doubt about what she'd say. The ladies trusted Aunt Camelia, who had a reputation as the finest psychic of her kind.

"It's Vica," Marius' grandmother exclaimed. "If anybody from the Security Services or Police comes in and wants to ask Vica any questions, her answer could clear the whole situation. She only needs to be smart enough to say that we, ahem, don't step outside the line in any way, right? She's the youngest woman among us. She's not tall either. We need to talk to Vica. Where's she?"

"She's out on a date," answered my aunt. "And it is not Vica. It is someone whose name begins with the letter D."

If the reading would have extended to encompass Marius' family, there would have been five people whose initials were D. But in our family, I was the only one whose name began with that letter. The jarring thought startled me. I gasped. Aunt Camelia shrieked. Marius' grandmother and at least one other lady jumped off their chairs.

"Speaking of the devil," said Grandma, lifting the table cloth.

Days went by. I began to believe that Aunt Camelia got it all wrong, and we were not in any danger at all. Moreover, good news was pouring in from all directions. Vica got engaged, and she was moving in with her fiancée at the end of the academic year. Our school won the literature contest, and our names were in the local newspapers. Marius made an unbelievable recovery, and his newly discovered interest in fitness and his athletic look made him very popular, especially among girls, which I loved teasing him about. On the last weekend before the end of the school year, we gathered at Marius house for a party, just our families, including Vica with her fiancée in tow, and Marius' cousins whom I met for the first time. Shy at first, they loosened up relatively quickly, and the five of us had a great time.

Whenever I thought that no one saw me, I looked furtively at Marius' family. His parents were so sweet to each other. I could say the same thing about his grandparents, whose daily bickering was rather fun than serious contention. I looked longingly at my own parents who, for the occasion, had put aside their differences. They even danced together for most of the evening. I felt hopeful. Maybe things would stay like that. Maybe their reconciliation was more than just a temporary truce. Maybe... Then, an empty feeling overtook me: among all the spells and charms that I knew, there wasn't even one that I could use to bring my parents together for good.

"It's too early even for the postman," Father said, while pausing his coffee to go open the door.

Voices drew near, then Father walked in the kitchen accompanied by four men: one dressed in uniform and the other three wearing civilian clothes.

"My name is Captain Cristescu. We have information about occult activities ongoing at this address, specifically cards reading, a practice that is subversive of the materialistic philosophy that governs our society. We have a written order to search the house and conduct inquiries with all the individuals living at this address." Captain Cristescu handed my father a piece of paper which he glanced over, signed, and handed back, saying:

"Oh, you made me worry. I thought there was something more serious. But, of course, we will do our best to help your investigation and clarify that this is a big misunderstanding."

The captain nodded curtly, then signaled two of his men to begin searching the house.

Captain Cristescu, I thought, had not only one C initial, but two. Handsome. Mustache. Really handsome. "When I get older, I guess I'll marry a guy in uniform," I told myself. One by one, my parents, grandma, Vica, went into the living room with the captain. The rest of us were waiting in the kitchen, seated around the table, with the third man dressed as a civilian watching over us. Mother offered him a chair, poured more coffee into Father's cup, and asked the guard if he would like some. He sat down with us, smiled politely and engaged in conversation with my parents. I thought he was friendly and probably a nice person. That was until he opened his jacket and I saw the gun in its holster. An alarm went off in my head: the bottle of water in my room, with herbs in it as it was, screamed of witchcraft from miles away. I felt sick. Grandma, the last one to be questioned, was still in the living room with Captain Cristescu, and even if she were with us, I couldn't say anything because of the guy guarding us. I felt a knot in my throat and my chin quivered. I was almost ready to cry. I didn't want anything bad to happen to Grandma and to any of us. I closed my eyes, squelching tears that ran down my cheeks.

"...a young person, stands on a teeter-totter. No wait: she stands on a scale. Depending on what she does, the scale will tip one way or the other." My aunt's voice resounded in my head. I wiped my face quickly, and looked at Father. His face was absolutely impenetrable, his demeanor calm, his whole being exuding confidence. Of course, that was the right way to handle the situation. I vowed to never in my life let fear get the best of me. I straightened my posture and held my head high just like my father. In trying to imitate him, I felt that somehow his confidence and self-assurance gradually transferred to me.

The door to the living room opened and Grandma walked out. Her gray-green eyes, cold like steel, met mine. I thought

I noticed a barely perceivable frown and a hint of a wink: was she trying to tell me something? Right behind her, the captain appeared in the doorframe.

"You," he pointed toward me, "would you like to chat with me a little while my assistants finish looking around the house? I'm getting bored here all by myself, and I believe we can have an interesting discussion. What do you say?" As he talked, a broad smile bloomed on the captain's face, sharply contrasting with his polite, yet cold, demeanor from only moments ago.

I nodded, stood up, and walked through the door held open by the captain. He politely pulled for me a chair at the table; probably the same chair that Grandma and everyone before her had sat on. Captain Cristescu stopped prowling. He sat down at the table across from me, asked again my name, which he wrote in a notebook, and continued to make conversation over trivia regarding school and my spare time. Without the warning brought about by Aunt Camelia's psychic inquiry and without all the all discussions and planning that followed, I would have fallen for the soft-spoken, mild-mannered, friendly-acting Captain Cristescu and trust him the way children trust authority figures, something which I would have had regretted for the rest of my life.

The captain pulled out of a pocket a deck of cards which he sat on the table.

"You are obviously very smart, so here's a question that I would appreciate your help with."

I tried to slow down my heart, pounding so hard that I believed it could be heard from across the room. "Powers that my Grandma calls upon, to whom I promised I'd be a useful friend forever, please help me," was the only thought I could entertain. I consciously focused on maintaining the same composure as my father although I found it a difficult enterprise. I wished for the captain to fire away his questions instead of painfully stretching that pause in conversation, which I felt was shredding my nerves.

Slowly, Captain Cristescu took the deck of cards out of the box and began shuffling with dexterity. Then he randomly pulled a few cards which he laid on the table face down. He turned one of the cards face-up, asking in a playful voice:

"What is this?"

"Ten of clubs." I was extremely careful about what I was saying, as Grandma had instructed me as soon as the ladies agreed that a threat was looming.

"Of course, that was easy. What about these then?" He turned the remaining cards face up, and I named them one by one.

"How would you read these?" Captain Cristescu made it sound more like a challenge rather than a question. On any other occasion I would have jumped at it and tried to read the cards as I had seen my aunt doing countless times. But I wasn't going to fall in that trap. I'll make Grandma proud. I'll keep us all safe. And when Granny would fully trust me, then she'll tell me about the Powers. I'll be a witch, maybe a witch that works with fairies, as I heard some medicine women do. The captain repeated his question.

"Read?" With new hope rose new enthusiasm. Fear vanished like smoke. "People read books, not cards. Was that a trick question?" I felt my heart regaining its usual tempo.

The captain seemed amused by my answer.

"Right, that was a trick question. But you know that there are people who pretend they can read cards actually? Have you ever heard of such a thing?"

That was uncomfortable. Very. A captain in the Security Services was asking me questions and I had to lie. Lie convincingly, because if not, my family would go to jail and I'd land in an orphanage: this is what Aunt Camelia said, and I had every reason to believe her. Our case would not have been singular, not by a long shot. I sighed, looked the captain straight in the eyes as I saw Father doing, and forced a little smile.

"No. I never heard of such a thing. I always read books, and play cards, captain."

"Do you? Do you really play cards?"

I nodded so hard that I thought my head would fall off. My enthusiasm made the captain chuckle.

"And what do you play?"

"Whist, Sixty-Six, Twenty-One, Pinnacle. I also play Rummy, I love it, although it's not cards."

"Wow, wow – these are not children's games. How do you know...Where did you learn these?"

"We play very often around here. I play with my parents, and I like to play with Grandma and her friends."

"Grandma and her friends? These are old ladies, aren't they? How did you end up hanging up with them to play cards?"

"Firstly, I am a really good player. Second, the ladies would be upset to hear that someone calls them old. Thirdly, they ask me each time they don't have a fourth person. Which means that I am playing a lot."

"Do they meet often?"

"They meet rather often. They are retired, like my grandmother, and have plenty of time on their hands. They play cards, drink tea, coffee, have snacks, tell stories, and play more cards."

"You must be a really good player for a group of retired women with a lot of card playing experience to ask you to join them, child." Captain Cristescu looked straight at me, his jaw set, almost confrontational. Another attempt to intimidate? I sustained his gaze.

"So you say... Here. Shuffle the cards," he said, handing me the deck.

The last bit of tension drained from me like the charge of a lightning bolt moving through a lightning rod and draining all the way into the ground. Everything that I said about playing cards with Grandma's friends was one hundred percent true. They always welcomed me to play, and only denied me access when they'd do witchy stuff, as per my parents' request. But that was not supposed to be part of my conversation with the captain.

My father was good at cards and strategy games. I learned from him how to play as much as I learned from Grandma. But Marius, he was the master, and eventually, weeks of keeping him company throughout his recovery turned me into a stronger player than I had ever been. I won the first two rounds, and Captain Cristescu won the third. He shook my hand, thanked me for keeping him company, and led me out of the room. The two men who searched the house were also there.

"Captain, we found these in the child's room." I panicked for a moment. The bottle of water that I had forgotten to remove from my room days ago when Grandma told me to do so, was now in the hands of those men.

The captain took the bottle and examined it.

"What is this? A magic brew, perhaps?"

Never in my whole life did my brain move that fast, not even during the literature contest from a month ago. Then I just heard myself talking:

"It's a cold infusion. I want to see how long it takes for the plants to flavor the water if left at room temperature as opposed to warming up on the stove. When it's ready, one can drink it," I said, knowing for a fact that the water in the bottle was perfectly safe to ingest.

The captain gave me back the bottle. I thanked him and put on display my most gracious smile.

"We also found this. It was in the child's bed, under the pillow." The man, who evidently searched my room, was holding the mugwort bunch Grandma had placed under my pillow for protection ever since I had the uncanny encounter in the woods.

The captain examined the little bundle.

"And this? Another experiment?"

"No, Captain. That's mugwort to protect against fleas," I said quickly.

"Against what?" The question almost exploded, propelled by a laughter outburst disguised as sudden cough.

"Flees," I said, "because, you see, I sleep with the cat."

Despite their best efforts, the Security men had the hardest of times to keep a straight face.

Then, Captain Cristescu read out loud his report according to which nothing was found in our house and on the surrounding premises to justify any of the allegations brought against us. Consequently, the captain himself recommended that any information regarding ongoing occult activities in our household be dismissed as false. He and the other three men then signed the report.

The captain sent his three subordinates to the car, while he stayed behind to talk with Father. Watching from the window, I could not hear what they were saying, but I saw my father smiling and nodding – which I thought, it could only be a good sign. As to confirm my feelings, the two men shook hands before parting.

But, upon coming back inside the house, Father insisted that we should not be fooled by the display of cordiality. While it might have been true that the captain had nothing personal against us and was glad to clear us of any accusation, we still could not ignore that he was, after-all, a military man carrying orders on behalf of a system that showed very little tolerance for insubordination. We ought to be careful because, according to my father, the house was probably still under surveillance. Although he spoke for everyone present, I felt that he was addressing me particularly.

Ever since Aunt Camelia sounded the alarm, the whole family prepared to face the worst. I had long talks with my family regarding the meaning of my aunt's predictions and about their implications, would those predictions come to pass. Even Father, so utterly dismissive of mystic, psychic, and occult stuff took my aunt's warning seriously. Grandma took care to eliminate everything that could have been held as proof, any kind of proof, against us. As such, she hung bunches of herbs inside her wardrobe: no one would tell off an old lady for using herbs instead of mothballs and air fresheners. Few other things that she kept in jars blended into the pantry among other cooking supplies and ingredients. Somehow, the bottle of cleansing water and the mugwort under my pillow slipped her attention and mine. I could not believe how that happened. The thought filled me with consternation. I had blown up my chance to prove myself one hundred percent responsible and therefore, reliable. How could I ever again ask Grandma to share with me her secrets and tune me into the Powers, when I had failed to carry out one simple set of instructions?

I was deeply torn between conflicting thoughts and feelings. That morning I entered the living room as a child, scared, dwarfed by the responsibility that I shouldered. I walked out as a mature person, head held high, as someone who battled and defeated the demons of fear and anguish tearing a child's heart. The more I thought of it, the more I felt my knees and stomach trembling. One wrong word, and the house search would have not ended with those cordial handshakes. I broke into a cold sweat. Really, no child should ever have to go through anything like this. For a short while I had believed that I grew, like heroes from fairy tales, several years in one day. That was until the man who searched my room came out with the bottle and the bunch of herbs. The illusion of greatness and growth popped then like a soap bubble. I sat there alone at the table, while everyone else was standing in the middle of the kitchen engaged in a very animated conversation. I expected a well-deserved rebuke. Then, Mother turned around and discovered my presence. In an outburst of emotion, she threw her arms around me, squeezing me hard.

"My wonderful child, the smartest, the brightest..." Her words melted into sobs, her hands patting my back and caressing my hair. I let it all sink in, then I joined into the sobbing. I didn't even know precisely why I was crying. Was the anxiety of the past hours getting the best of me? Was I beating myself up for having been neglectful? Was I just being moved by my mom's unfiltered outpour of affection? Was the bitter-sweet appearance of togetherness mixed with the knowing that my parents had never been farther apart from each other as they were at the moment?

"I have never heard of Odysseus crying." It was all it took to get my tears to stop and bring my emotions back under control. I stood up tall and took the hand that my father offered. A hand shake, a pat on the back, a short but strong hug, a wink, that sense of partnership that always made me feel important and responsible for my decisions and their outcomes: my relationship with my father, in a nutshell.

Chapter 14

I woke up with the sunlight coloring my bed sheet pale pink. The early morning breeze made the light sheers float. I closed my eyes again hoping to bring back, even briefly, the green hills, the meadow dotted with bright yellow flowers, the immense blue sky above the landscape I had wandered through in my dream. It was a recurrent dream, always ending with me running toward the hill where a rectangular opening into its side allured me to explore. I always woke up when I was either just about to step in, or a few feet away from it. The dream felt painfully real, and it triggered a longing that I could not explain. Sometimes, I couldn't wait to fall asleep, hopeful that I'll dream the same dream again. The sun shone brighter. Rays tickled my face, making me giggle. I'd try to dream it again later.

During breakfast, I shared about my dream, about the sense of happiness, safety, about feeling literally at home in that emerald green meadow. I wondered out loud how it would feel to actually reach the hill. What would I find behind the little rectangular gate if I were to enter it? I wanted to know if there was actually a way to determine what to dream about, because if such a thing existed, I really wanted to know about it. I had to reach the hill and answer the call to go past the gate.

Father took the opportunity to give me a crash course in psychology. He explained that dreams are ways for the body to process the emotional and mental baggage coming from different events. Father explained that such processing was a necessary step for people to maintain mental and physical health. I shrugged my shoulders, only half convinced by what I heard. Aunt Camelia had told me once that many dreams contain messages about future events. Some other times, spirits of all sorts reach out to us in dreams, and those encounters that occur in a dream state are as valid as any encounter one would have while awake. I waited for my father to leave to work, and I shared my thoughts with Grandma and Vica. Vica jumped in eagerly to confirm everything I just said. She had heard the same thing from her own grandmother, and always slept with holy basil under her pillow which she marked with the sign of cross every time she went to sleep.

"Why the holy basil and the cross sign," I asked.

"To keep away any demon or malicious spirit that could come into my dreams," Vica said. "And I sprinkle holy water around the room," she added cheerfully, as if somebody was about to hand her a badge of honor for diligent answering.

I made a face... Sprinkling holy water in her room: no wonder that the curse intended to send her packing took so long to work.

Grandma also made a face, but for a completely different reason:

"Aunt Camelia needs to talk less," was her comment. "And about your dream, as long as it's not a nightmare that doesn't let you rest properly, I am not concerned."

I had a different feeling though, and I planned to actually talk to my aunt at the first opportunity.

I didn't have to wait too long. Aunt Camelia came over that afternoon. Before everyone gathered in Grandma's quarters, I found the time to talk to her about my dream.

"Maybe it's just a nice dream," was her first reaction. "If it makes you feel good, just enjoy it."

"Auntie, I've been having this dream repeatedly. It's like that place is calling for me. Being in the meadow by the hill feels amazing, but not being able to reach the opening in its side leaves me so frustrated!"

I saw my aunt frowning, a sure sign that she took my words seriously.

"Here's what I think about your dream. I believe that the meadow and joy that you feel is just yourself finding peace after these very difficult months" The uncertainty on my face prompted her to explain further.

"The tensions between your parents, the Security questioning the whole family – it is a lot for a child to take in. Your dream may be your own body healing." That sounded a lot like what my father said. I opened my mouth to say what I thought, but I closed it back quickly, because my aunt continued. "There may be the case that the dream has a deeper meaning. The opening that you can't reach may indicate something that you want badly, something hovering right at your fingertips, and when you are just about to get it, it slips farther away. Hills are also connected to some fairies. This hill may also be a real place that you'll get to visit one day, and you'll find out more about it in due time.

I nodded vigorously.

"You are right about me wanting something that I seemingly can't get no matter how much I try."

"And what would that be?"

I swallowed hard, and after a moment of hesitation I popped my question:

"What are the Powers that Grandma works with? I know a lot about what she does, like spells and charms for healing, protection, and so on. But she calls on Powers, and there are things she's doing and doesn't want to share. I'm dying to know what all this is about. Also, I want to know more about fairies, but she won't say much either."

"Have you asked her? "

I nodded again, even more vigorously than before.

"Of course, I did, many times. She won't tell me anything though, and insists that I have to wait until I'm a little older. Can you help me? Please!!"

My aunt took me by the hand, and drew me closer. She put her arm around my shoulders.

"I was exactly like you, wanting to know everything at once. It turned out that learning charms and spells before learning self-mastery is a very, very bad idea. You already know much more than I knew when I was your age. Your mom never cared about magic or folk medicine, and believe me, she's a much happier person than I am." I had my own doubts about that, but I didn't say anything.

Aunt Camelia continued: "I was never interested in those Powers, and even when your grandmother explained those to me, I could not connect. Now I work with angels. They are powerful, act as protectors, as agents of revenge, they also bring about healing, and intercede to God for me. They are not the powers your grandmother speaks about, but maybe you would like to connect with angels – why not? I can help you."

"Nah. I don't feel drawn toward angels. I'm into fairies, but I don't really know how to approach them outside the seasonal rituals, you know, the ones that we do around their holidays, Rusalii and Sânziene[16]. This year was so exciting, because Grandma and I did the welcoming of zâne, right around Easter time. My mom wasn't super-pleased but Grandma had it her way, and mine."

"Well, I believe that you have to listen to your granny then. Just be good and patient, and she'll tell you all that you need to know."

While it wasn't exactly the answer that I wanted, I enjoyed the conversation with my aunt. I got my place around the table. Aunt Camelia winked as she handed me the deck of cards.

"The person to the left cuts; the game moves to the right," I announced, and began to shuffle.

Chapter 15

The moonlight filled up the room. The light curtains moved in the breeze that made the treetops whisper. It was almost midnight but sleep was not part of my plans. That night, I was set to discover the best guarded yet among grandma's secrets. I wasn't doing it out of sheer curiosity. Grandma's work concerned me in more ways than I could even tell. I hid behind curtains, hoping to see...

Something moved right near my right arm startling me. I almost jumped, forgetting that I was perched on a windowsill on the second floor. Two fiery dots were fixating me. I ignored the purring. I could distinguish the sound of someone's fumbling with the lock at the backdoor. So, she'd come out soon. I looked over my shoulder to the clock on the wall: two phosphorescent sides dragged themselves to narrow an angle, slowly, tugging at my nerves. Wasn't yet the time? I heard the door opening. "Meow!" I reached quickly to pet the cat needy for attention, and to prevent more meowing that would have, no doubt, made Grandma look our way. My hand froze in midair. Grandma, who had barely stepped outside, stared straight up at my room's window. Only a few times in my life did I wish more fervently to be invisible. An eternity went by. Finally, Grandma began walking toward the apple tree, and I breathed again. I noticed that she carried two baskets, one on each arm. When she reached the apple tree, grandma put the baskets down.

I saw her taking out a napkin which she laid on the ground; the white piece of cloth shone silver in the moonlight. She took out more things, and I grew frustrated because I couldn't see what they were. She was there on her knees for a while, then I saw her holding up a bottle. The purring had stopped and in that perfect silence I heard the sound of liquid pouring into cups. What was that? Was Grandma having a nocturnal picnic?

128

That is not what I heard, spying again, of course, that she'd be doing. She got up and moved a little closer in my direction. I saw her standing in the open space between the house, the apple tree, and the herbs garden. I looked past the garden, toward the woods. The breeze died; the stillness and quiet felt unreal.

Grandma's voice broke the silence. She was humming a melody that, albeit sounding familiar, I didn't know if I had actually heard it before. She moved in a sort of dance, her steps tracing a circle. I couldn't see her face, but I could somehow sense her excitement. She was dancing, turning and spinning, sometimes faster and sometimes slower. Her apron came loose, but she didn't notice. I had no idea how long it passed since her dancing had begun. I only knew that I wanted so much to be there with her and do what she was doing – whatever that was.

It had been a while. Watching Grandma turning endlessly around an invisible circle had a hypnotic effect. I felt my eyes closing. "No! No, no – you can't fall asleep on the windowsill," I told myself, mildly alarmed at the perspective of what could happen. And most importantly, who knew when would I have another chance to find out about Grandma's whereabouts, that she won't tell me anything about? I knew that she's a doftoroaie[17], a very good one. I knew that people still came to her for help. I wanted to be like her, and I believe she still enjoyed passing down her teaching onto me. I always had a sense of knowing that there was more to what she did, but she was adamant in keeping me away. "Not yet," came her answer whenever I pressed on with questions. "You are too young for this," which drove me mad, because I was almost ten years old.

I thought about the encounter I had with the girl who at first, seemed to be a child like myself; our short meeting, fleetingly passing by one another and her vanishing in the woods. I remembered that something felt unusual about her. I still could not tell whether it was her clothes, the fact that she ran so unbelievably fast, or the way she had me follow her deep into the woods. I still believed that Grandma exaggerated in her precautions. We had gathered into my room, and together we crafted a small pouch that I had to wear all the time. She said the red cloth and red ribbon of the pouch along with the mugwort, basil, and ashes in it would protect me against any malevolent spirits and fairies. "Malevolent fairies? Aren't fairies nice to children," I had asked. I had my Fairy Ed 101 right there and then. The first thing that I learned was that fairies can be nice, even a little bit too nice to children whom they may try to lure away; once in Fairy, such children may not be able to return home anymore. "But I'm not afraid," I had said. "I know that I can be friends with the fairies, and they wouldn't harm me." I remembered Grandma's eyes growing wide as if she'd seen a ghost. For months afterwards, she kept a strict eye on me each time I'd go outside to play. Some days, she'd even take along her sewing or knitting, and hang around, for as long as I was outside. None of these bothered me except the fact that Grandma still surrounded a certain part of her work with a thick wall of secrecy which made me all the more curious and stubbornly nosy.

Not long ago, I had heard Grandma, my mom, and my aunt talking about a ritual to be done on the first night of the full moon. I had gotten all the information eavesdropping, of course. However, none of them said clearly when the first night of full moon would actually occur. I was left to guess, and for a couple of weeks, my parents noticed my newly discovered interest in astronomy and moon phases. And there I was, staring from behind curtains.

Grandma stopped dancing. She stood with her arms raised, facing the apple tree, and chanted:

"Zânelor prea-bunelor..."[18]

Zâne?? I shuddered. Did the lighting strike? Was my grandmother a Soimancă[19]? The recitation continued, and I was both in awe and paralyzed by surprise. I looked around the backyard, at the woods, the apple tree, hungrily taking in every detail...What's that? Long and slender silhouettes glowing silvery in the moonlight glided by grandmother's picnic: a flash going on and off. Did I really see them? Were those...? My heart was about to leap out of my chest. I never wanted anything so badly but to do what Grandma was doing. I didn't know why and I didn't even care. I wanted to be a witch and make friends with the fairies. I watched Grandma slowly walking away toward the apple tree, picking up the second basket, then disappearing in the herbs garden. My eyes followed her with a mix of admiration, love, and envy. A lot of envy.

I dropped onto my bed, nearly smashing the cat. Although I was dead tired, I couldn't fall asleep. I had known about Soimance, fairy witches or fairy doctors, but never thought that my own grandmother was one of them. So that was her secret which, for whatever the reason, she didn't want to share with me. Fine by me, I thought. If she would not teach me fairy witchcraft, I was determined to figure it out by myself. I knew enough of the 'witchy' to discover the 'fairy' part on my own.

I kept my eyes shut tightly, reluctant to open them and get out of bed. The night before... The night before? "MY PLAN," my mind bellowed. I was out of bed and into my clothes probably even before opening my eyes completely.

It was almost noon when I stepped out of the house carefully, making sure that nobody saw me. The last thing that I wanted is being questioned over the pile of things I have gathered and carried in my arms like trophies. I snuck behind the herb garden. There's my place: a small patch of grass between wild roses and blackthorns. I often went there to read or play by myself. It felt enchanted, it always did, but it felt even more so on that day. I was ready.

I stepped toward the center of the space, the cloak – Grandma's burgundy velvet tablecloth – trailing behind me. I felt sweat dripping off my back, and I'm quite sure it was not just because of the weather outside. I advanced solemnly holding the basket (yes, one of those that Grandma used the night before), and stopped by one of the blackthorns. I laid down the towel I stole from the kitchen, and on top of it I arranged neatly three cups: one for water, one containing a handful of cherries, and a third one filled with chocolate candy. Then I took out my most precious possessions. Next to the cups, I placed my two favorite books and my best ink pen. Near the towel, I laid the bow and a few arrows that Dad gave me, and my wooden sword. I was very pleased. I thought that Grandma would be very proud, only if... OK. I had to stay focused.

I did not know how to dance the way I saw Grandma dancing, so I twirled around in a choreography of my own making. I whistled a tune that I had learned at school and which I thought befitted the occasion. The "cloak" floated and waved around my body as I moved, and for some reason that filled me up with a sense of importance. I was getting dizzy from spinning, so I stopped. Standing in the middle of the space, I cleared my throat and in the most solemn tone that I could master, I recited:

"Zânelor prea-bunelor..."

I only remembered the first two lines of Grandma's oration, so I went on improvising the rest. I was a nervous wreck, but gradually my heart slowed down. I reached a level of comfort where I began making requests to the zâne that I invited to the table that I had prepared for them.

"Bless my books to always be my teachers, to tell me all I need to know about fairies and fairy witchcraft, because my granny won't tell me anything. Bless my pen to write perfect assignments and always bring home good grades. Bless my bow and arrows..."

"And what are you going to give in exchange for these blessings?" Grandmother's voice made me freeze. "Before making more requests, think about what do you have to offer to the fairies in exchange. If you seek a partnership you have to give, not only take. You are a witch, not a beggar. Watch carefully the words coming out of your mouth, because agreements made with fairies are binding. Don't lie, and don't pretend," she continued. The silence grew heavy, and I felt silly. Of course, the fairies should get something in exchange, duh! Even if they liked me – which I always assumed was the case – it would still be nice on my side to give something in return. But what? The sense of importance and greatness from only moments ago, disintegrated. I felt shrinking under the cloak which, all of a sudden, seemed too big and heavy on my tiny body. I turned around and faced Grandma. I saw her gaze scrutinizing everything. I wondered how much of my own version of the fairy-invoking ritual she had witnessed. Grandma answered my thoughts. "Not bad, not bad at all," she said, pointing with her chin to the towel and the things on it. "I see that you are wearing the pouch that we made, which tells me that you take these... things seriously." I nodded. "What can I offer in exchange for their blessings? How do I become a fairy witch like yourself," I heard myself begging. I would never forget the look on Grandma's face when she spoke again.

"I have to teach you a few things at least, because it is probably the best way to keep you safe. I didn't want to, but you give me no choice. However, whether you'll become a fairy witch or not, whether they will choose you as a working partner or not, I cannot tell. It's entirely up to them."

I smiled. I knew they would. I could not tell where this 'knowing' was coming from, but I felt it right in my heart. I didn't say anything to Grandma, except asking for her help to finish the ritual.

We faced the blackthorn in whose shade I had set up my things. Grandma stood behind me, her hands on my shoulders. Our voices united:

"Zânelor prea-bunelor…"

She led and I followed. I felt happier than I had ever been in my entire life. Ahead of me a path just opened, a path that only in my wildest dreams I dreamed of walking: a fairy path.

Chapter 16

For the next few days, I basked in my own glory. I expected something magnificent and glorious to happen at some point. After all, Grandma had just formally initiated me into her practice, right? But nothing was actually happening, nothing that I was aware of.

"Now what?" The question itself felt so dull as I pondered over it!

I went to talk to Grandma, who over the past days acted as if she didn't even have a recollection of the fact that she had just initiated me into becoming a fairy seer.

"What do you think you should be doing now?" Grandma answered my question with another question of her own. I thought hard, but nothing came to mind, nothing that I could have considered an active step into my apprenticeship. Was I supposed to engage now with fairies every day? And if yes, then how? I said nothing, just shrugged my shoulders. Grandma chuckled. "Well, you will do almost the same things that you did until now, just with more consistency and focus. You will also have to actively and regularly show respect to Them. Remember, these are Powers that we are talking about. All zâne are powerful, and their queens are even more so. At this time *your* job is to show respect and a desire to work alongside Them."

"And how exactly am I supposed to do all these," I asked before even Grandma could draw her breath between sentences.

"You will do your room warding, once a week. You will use the water from the bottle, and as you asperse the room you will intend for Mugwort to keep away all inimical beings, allowing the goodly inclined ones to come near. Listen carefully. You are to be as specific as possible about who you want to keep away and who you want to allow near you. I will help you at first, but you must learn to do it on your own. It's not easy and it is risky. Are you still with me?"

I nodded. I still could not believe that dealing with fairies would be as risky as Grandma was making it sound, and I believed that she was just trying to add extra protective layers so the overly-enthusiastic me wouldn't get into any real danger. I didn't share my thoughts though, and Grandma, visibly pleased with my attention, continued:

"You will also leave offerings for zâne once a week, by the blackthorn that I noticed you feel drawn to. Consider that a sacred space dedicated to Them. You could go there to read, think, contemplate, hold rituals, work magic, and of course, make offerings. You are not going to treat that space like a playground though, and you must keep its meaning secret. This is for you, and only for you." Grandma said her last words with added oomph. I liked the way it sounded, I liked to have my own space, build my own relationship, but on the other hand, the thought that one day I will just let go of the training wheels felt both elating and scary.

"Just once a week? Only in the garden? I believe I saw you offering to them more often than this, at least occasionally. And if I am not mistaken, I saw you leaving food on the windowsill in your room. Is that too, for fairies?"

Grandma clapped her hands in surprise. She laughed a hearty laugh.

"Is there anything that you don't notice? You will do offerings only by the blackthorn for a while. We will see what happens, how are your offerings being received, and take omens regularly to see how do the zâne regard you."

I must have looked confused and probably funny, because Grandma's smile grew wider, as I continued to inquire.

"But I was initiated the day you walked me through the ritual, hands on my shoulders, and then explained to me the fairies as the Powers that you call upon when you do your work, the powers that teach, protect, assign tasks, and occasionally challenge us. Isn't that enough? Why do we need to take omens to see how do the fairies regard me? Am I not one of the people working alongside them?"

"If it were so simple, my dear child... First of all, you want to make sure that you start on the right foot, and this means getting on their good side. Think of it this way: how would you feel if a person whom you met only once or twice in a formal setting would burst into your house next day and demand that you share your knowledge and give them your time and energy for something that only benefits them? Now imagine that the same person gets into the habit of pestering you with questions and requests all the time, feeling entitled to demand that you always answer. How would you feel?"

"I'd punch them in the face," I answered without even thinking. It seemed outrageous that somebody, anybody, would try to exploit me like that.

"Oh, I believe you, and I completely understand. I would chase them with the broom," Grandma chuckled as she mimicked the action to my greatest amusement.

"Well," she continued, "we wouldn't want you to be that rude and annoying person knocking at the fairies' doors, would we?"

"You mean... Oh, I believe I got it. First, I need to approach them respectfully, introduce myself with more than just stating my name, letting them know me and that I really want to make friends..."

"Yes, my dear; you want them to know that you are not there just to ask for things and take advantage as you would treat milking a cow. You have to offer something in return. Relationships with fairies, like most relationships, are quite transactional. Remember what I asked you the first time, when you were just requesting one blessing after another?"

"Yeah, you told me that I am a witch, not a beggar. I had offerings for Them, though. I wasn't begging.'

"If you have friends coming over for dinner, would you ask them for favors in exchange for the meal you invited them for?"

"That would be horrible. I never meant it that way. Wow, so offerings to zâne are just like having guests for dinner and I'd honor them with the best hospitality that I can provide. I shall be happy for the guests coming over and not because I'd have a chance to ask them for favors. Now I understand what offerings are about."

"And, after some time, when the relationship acquires depth, they may offer protection, might begin to give you gifts such as advice on how to do healing work or solve problems. This relationship takes a long time to build. So, be honest with yourself about the reason you are seeking it, in the first place."

I was enthralled. Yet I had no precise answer to the question about my own motivation to seek the relationship with fairies. As I thought of it, I didn't want to gain anything concrete from it. I wasn't seeking a tit for tat kind of relationship, rather, I just wanted to be friends. Not that I would have minded gifts coming from them, but at the same time I thought that I wanted that connection even if nothing more tangible came out of it. It was like being accepted around the big dogs: just hanging around with the pack was a reward in itself.

I told Grandma what I thought. Her smile brightened the space around us.

"This is good, very good. You are coming at this from the right place. Zâne bless and protect the ones they chose, but when this would happen, there's no telling. Let's go out and make an offering right now. You'll do it while I'll watch to make sure nothing is left out."

I decided to keep things simple. I sliced an apple and put it on a small plate along with a spoonful of honey. I poured water in a cup, and some milk in another. I gathered everything on a tray.

"Where are you going," Grandma asked, surprised to see that I was heading upstairs to my room.

"My pouch," I answered, "and, uh, something else."

Grandma patted me on the back, sighed seeing the red pouch, and smiled at the wand that I brought with me. She continued to talk as we walked toward the blackthorn in the backyard.

"As far as the pouch goes, you don't need it in these kinds of circumstances. It was made to keep away anyone among Themselves who is not goodly inclined toward you. But you now invite around yourself those among the Powers who are benevolent and willing to partake from what you offer. Sometimes, you'll need the protection pouch and some other times, you won't. And what do you want to do with that wand?"

"I don't know exactly, but I had the urge to bring it with me. Is it wrong? Do you ever use a wand?"

"It is not wrong, assuming that you have in mind a clear purpose for it, because otherwise, you'll end up carrying around all kinds of useless things, just for décor, just to show that you are a medicine woman, or a witch, or whatever you choose to call yourself. I don't use fancy wands, just sticks rather, different kinds of wood, depending on the work that I do. For the most part, however, I don't."

"What are your wands made of?"

"I have twigs of apple, hazel, and hawthorn – don't start chopping branches off trees to make wands. This is knowledge that I got from Them, over time. Remember that for your wand, you found the pine twig? I'd say that most times you will find the wood that you need, just lying around. Some other times, you'll have to harvest it. One of these days I'll show you how to do that. Now please think of what you can do with your wand, if anything. And if you find no use for it, next time you do offerings, don't bring the wand along."

We arrived by my blackthorn. I put down the tray, then stood up fidgeting with my wand. In the breeze that picked up, a few leaves twirled forming a miniature whirlwind that swept the ground as it passed just near us. I felt my face stretching in a glorious grin as I began turning counterclockwise, spiraling from the center of the space outward, the wand like a lightning rod held high above my head. Out loud, I intended for the space to open up and the gates between our world and theirs' to swing open signaling to zâne our invitation. I stopped facing the blackthorn, and sent a furtive look over the shoulder to check for signs, if any, coming from my grandmother. Seeing her nod, barely perceivable, I went on to leave the offerings on the flat stone that I had carried there a few days before, specifically for this purpose. I cleared my throat, and recited the invocation which I could remember only partly. Whatever I couldn't remember, I improvised, since Grandma herself had said that words have power when they come straight from the heart. Then, we sat down in silence, looking and listening. Suddenly, birds burst into song. The blackthorn's leaves rustled. My senses devoured every bit of input from around us, yet my mind was somehow floating, suspended, unable and unwilling to form thoughts: getting drunk with sensation was plenty.

Once a week I'd leave offerings for zâne by the blackthorn. In talking with Grandma about fairies and trees, I had found out that I was the only person she knew being attracted to blackthorn. Apple trees, pear trees, beeches, birches, and hawthorns were the customary places to leave offerings for zâne on their holidays, not blackthorns. I sometimes accompanied Grandma by the apple tree that she favored, but whenever I was by myself, the blackthorn was my default place to go. It wasn't only for offerings: it was one of my favorite places where I'd go to read, draw, play, or lay on my back and do nothing else but watch the sky changing colors at sunset, clouds chasing each other on breezy days, or stars twinkling on an indigo-blue backdrop. It was my place to seek solace when my heart ached, which happened increasingly more often given that the tension between my parents was mounting.

It was during one such argument when I grabbed a cup of water and the sandwich I had just made for myself and ran outside to my blackthorn. Albeit hungry, I couldn't bear Mother and Father's shouts resounding throughout the house; it made each morsel of food get stuck in my throat. I walked fast, yet careful not to spill the content of the cup. I sat down by the hedge, where the shade was deep enough to keep me out of the merciless afternoon sun. I pulled out of my pocket a deck of cards, intending to entertain myself with a game of Solitaire. But then, I got an idea. Why not read cards, like Aunt Camelia? If such gifts run in the family, and if the resemblance Grandma said I bore to my aunt was real, then maybe I was also a gifted psychic. I quickly selected the twenty-four cards which I knew were needed for reading, and began to shuffle. I had plenty to think of, many questions needing an answer, so I forgot about food, at least for the moment.

"Don't do it," a child's voice resounded clear and quite loud. My hands froze in midair, a few cards falling randomly in the grass. I looked in the direction of the voice, but my eyes met nothing but the blackthorn. I tentatively shuffled again while looking around to find out who spoke. Nothing happened, so I pulled a card from the deck, laid it down, and looked at it carefully. I was taken aback by the unsettled, raw feeling it raised within me, a state bordering on anxiety. "Really, no," I heard the voice again. I lifted my eyes quickly, to catch a glimpse of the speaker before its eventual disappearance. In defiance of my expectations, the familiar face did not run away, nor did it disappear. She was dressed the same as the day we first met, except for the garland of white flowers she wore on her head. She looked at me gravely, and right then it dawned on me what was odd about her: her chestnut brown eyes were not a child's eyes. If it was true that the eyes are windows to someone's soul, I could swear that the pair staring at me had seen a lot more life than me or anyone that age. I was split between the impulse of going straight to her, and the awareness that I did not fully understand what was going on, and therefore of potential danger. I remained seated, and wondered what would happen if she'd come closer. As if answering my thought, the girl took a couple of steps in my direction. The sunlight shone on her, or off her – I couldn't really tell – making her seem material and immaterial at the same time. Inexplicably, the apprehensive feeling from moments ago flaked away, being replaced by an almost bubbly, joyful state.

"Hi! I never thought I'd see you again," I said, stretching out my hand which she didn't take. The girl remained standing, shifting her weight from one foot to the other, her gaze sizing me up. I could not explain what happened next, who or what prompted me to act the way I did. As I stood up, the deck of cards slid from my lap and scattered on the ground. I took the cup of water and the sandwich, and walked toward the blackthorn. I advanced, maintaining what I believed to be a safe distance from the girl. I put the cup on the flat stone, broke the sandwich in half and left one piece near the cup. Then I returned to my place.

"What's your name," I asked, without any real hope she'd even answer.

"You know that I always wear white, don't you?"

I shrugged my shoulders and nodded at the same time, feeling confused by the ambiguity of my own gesture.

"Why should I not read cards?"

"Don't. It's not for you."

"What? What do you mean? I'm not any less than my aunt."

"Yes. You are not any less. You are more than you think you are. If you read those, you put yourself in danger. It is not for you."

"Why should I believe you? I don't even know who you are."

The dark brown eyes grew immense for a moment then narrowed to slits in the next one.

"You know who I am. Trust yourself. Embrace your knowing. Do not read cards like your aunt. It is not for you. Other ways, yes. Some day."

I was getting dizzy. I could hear the words coming from her as she spoke, but I could also hear them inside my head. If not for the doctors having meticulously checked my brain and finding it perfectly normal, I would have screamed and declared that I've gone crazy. And the girl, who before I wanted to play with, I now wished her gone. I closed my eyes, and hoped that upon opening them again I'd no longer see her. But she was still there, looking at me, asking whether I would do as she advised. I nearly blew a fuse. Who on earth was she to lecture me like that? Even with those mature-looking eyes, she wasn't any figure of authority who could tell me what to do. Strange as she was, she was nothing but a kid like myself. I opened my mouth to speak. She raised her arm with the index finger lifted, demanding silence. I felt as if her index finger sealed my lips, albeit not touching them. Then she vanished.

When I got inside the house I was shaking. My hands were icy cold and my teeth were chattering. Cold sweat ran down my back. It took me a while to gather my breath, words, and composure, and tell Grandma about the encounter that I just had. After thoroughly checking on me to eliminate the possibility of a heatstroke, Grandma spoke with a mix of resignation and reproach:

"I hope that you finally understand the reasons why we wait until people reach a certain maturity before being initiated into fairy seership. I am surprised how fast your relationship to zâne is evolving. In a sense, I feel better that I began teaching you despite your age. I realized that at least, you gain a real understanding of what fairy partnerships involve, and that knowledge may keep you safer than ignorance. You have been placed under a prohibition that you are bound to honor. If you don't, you are in big trouble. You can see for yourself that things are quite different from what nowadays children's books say about fairies."

We walked back to the blackthorn. On the stone, a greasy spot marked the place where the piece of sandwich stood earlier. I picked up the cup from where I had left it and poured out the water, inviting the spirits of the place and the goodly inclined among the fairies to receive it. When I finished, I looked around for signs and omens – as Grandma taught me. On the ground, right in front of me lay a twig with a few leaves and thorns. I had nearly stepped on it.

"Grandma, look! I have a new wand," I said while picking up the blackthorn twig.

"Wait. You still have time to back off. Leave the twig here alongside new offerings, and prepare an explanation as to why you are not engaging any further. I'll back you up. But if you choose to accept the gift, the twig, then you may be entering this partnership in a more formal and therefore more binding way. I'd say that you wait. On the other hand, if the fairies are really set on you, and you also have the desire to pursue, then me holding you back would attract their animosity, which is even worse. So, make up your mind please."

I put the twig down where I found it, and paced around for a while. Great, I thought. At my age children were required to begin thinking about future professions, and explore interests that would help them build in that direction. They'd have months and years to figure things out. I had less than one day's time to make up my mind about entering a life-long relationship with fairies.

"Nah. I'm all in." I bent over, and picked up my wand-to-be.

"How is the new wand coming along?" I nodded slightly, absorbed in the crafting, while Grandma watched as I removed the thorns and leaves off the twig. I only had to smoothen the ends a little, and I'd be done. Grandmother had asked me to pay close attention to what I feel, and what thoughts come through while I was working on my wand. In following her advice, I had found myself talking to the blackthorn twig quite a lot.

The house was quiet. Vica, who came back to town just the day before, rushed to see her boyfriend. My parents, in the aftermath of their argument, went out to the movies together, one of those inconsistencies in their interactions that shredded my nerves to pieces. It broke my heart to hear them arguing and threatening to separate, and then, hours later, they'd be going out together like nothing had ever happened. Oftentimes Mother would almost deny that they'd had any conflict, and she'd keep a happy face on, until Father would leave on his next business trip, during which time she'd bitch about what a terrible man he was. The reading that I had attempted earlier was aimed at gaining some clarity about my parents' relationship, and hopefully save my sanity. I felt trapped in the conflict between Mother and Father, trapped by the need to pick a side, so when they'd fall apart, I shall not be left on the outside. However desperate for information, I was not going to tempt my luck and read cards against the fairy's prohibition. Thinking of my parents' convoluted marriage made me anxious. I was embarrassed to tell Grandma how I felt though, for fear of being seen as weak and unfit, for apprenticing with her.

I finished sanding the ends of the twig, peeled only a little bit of bark to mark the "handle", and putting a little spittle on the bottom end, I said: "We are now one." I immediately felt immensely relieved, as if a powerful shield placed itself between me and my anxiety. "Whatever my parents do, don't do, or will do, I'll be just fine." The thought just floated through, softly and comforting.

I bundled up three thorns and tied them together with black thread. "Blackthorn, my friend, take care of me and I'll take care of you," I addressed what I believed to be the spirit of Blackthorn, while I wrapped the bundle of thorns in a small piece of cloth. I put the bundle into my pocket. I had every reason to believe that the way I felt was no different than the way knights felt when putting on suits of armor. Then, I gathered the few leaves and the remaining thorns in a blue glass ashtray which I took to my room. I could swear on the efficiency of the blackthorn protection charm that I had just made. But that prompted another thought. What was then the best way to protect against inimical beings without chasing away or even worse, angering the ones to whom I was seeking to connect?

Grandma and I sat down for dinner, just the two of us. I didn't feel like talking. I had an awful lot to think of and the words simply could not keep up with my thoughts. I finally asked Grandma about how to create protections that were selective.

"First and foremost, strengthen the bonds with the beings that you want to be with in a clique, so to speak; they will defend against less friendly beings, should you ever run in with any of those. It is like having good friends among people in positions of power. As you advance in your practice, and if you are lucky, a fairy queen or king might take you under their wing. Then you would have little to fear but a whole lot more work to do and obligations to fulfill. And as soon as you'd put a toe outside the line, the repercussions could be severe."

I sighed and looked at Grandma, as if seeing her for the first time. The outpouring of love that I felt coming from her was almost overwhelming. I was overjoyed to receive it yet squelched under the pressure of deserving it. I didn't want anything for free, I wanted everything, including affection to be merit-based. I realized that it was good training in dealing with fairies too. If I'd apply myself seriously, I'll work my way up to deserving their friendship and trust, and if they deem me worthy, they'd bestow on me their magical knowledge. I felt very confident that I could get myself there. I shared my last thought with Grandma.

"It's good thinking. Show respect, do not offend them, and do not act entitled, because they don't owe anything to us."

I piled up more French fries on my plate.

"Grandma, and how does one know they are in the good graces of a Fairy queen?"

"She'll let that person know. They are usually direct."

"And what if no queen ever takes interest in a doftoroaie, seer, or whatever?"

"Fairies are numerous in kind and number. It may not be a Fairy queen who partners up directly with a seer, but every seer has one or more close guides among fairies. It is like having one or more reliable friends who provide assistance, and to whom, in turn, one should reciprocate."

I hesitated, but in the end, curiosity got the best of me:

"Grandma, do you have a Fairy queen that you work with?"

"The short answer is, yes. And I also have other guides among fairies, but please don't ask me for any more details."

I wasn't going to ask for any more details, not right away anyway. I asked instead for another slice of the chocolate cake that Grandma had made especially for me.

Vica entered the kitchen, smiling and twirling. She hugged Grandma, put on an apron, rolled up her sleeves, and took over the sink full of dishes.

"Oh, glad to see that I arrived just in time."

Standing next to her, Grandma dried the dishes one by one that Vica washed and rinsed. My job was to pick up the dry dishes and put them in the cupboards. I gathered they were discussing Vica's boyfriend, and I believed to have heard the word fiancée.

"What? This means you are about to get married, right?" I butted into the discussion, overjoyed by the news. If Vica married, she'd move in with her husband, and I'd be rid of her. Grandma didn't seem to share my enthusiasm. She was undoubtedly happy for Vica, but also felt sorry she'd leave us.

I went upstairs. I was tired and ready to go to bed. I turned off the lights and opened the window to let in the feeble breeze of the July night. Stunned, I watched my parents strolling in the backyard... holding hands. I wanted to laugh and cry at once. Feeling heartbroken over the argument they had had earlier suddenly appeared silly and nonsensical. Yet, I could not allow myself to be happy either. The romantic moment I was witnessing could burst anytime like a soap bubble, and I'd plummet again from the heights of happiness into the depth of grief. Anxious anticipation inched in. When would the next argument break out? Tonight? In the morning? Next week? I reached for the little bundle of thorns, my protection charm. My anxiety began to dissolve, same as it did earlier that evening, Blackthorn told me that I'd be safe whatever my parents would do or not do. I began to wonder if there was anything that I could do magically to make them stay together and get along. Before finally going to sleep, I made a mental note to ask Grandma about a love charm that I could use on my parents, if such a thing existed.

Chapter 17

"I am reminding you, that these are not the kind of fairies that you read about in children's fairytales, or the ones in the cartoons you may be watching," Grandma said sternly, as she was getting dressed.

"I know, and I am coming with you. Am I your apprentice, or not?"

"Then hurry up. Make sure that you carry your protection charms."

We left the room that Grandma and I were sharing in the house of Vica's parents where we were visiting. We entered the living room where two women were waiting. The older woman pointed toward me:

"What are you doing, dear? You should be in bed."

"I'm coming to help," I answered, and straightened my back to look taller. I patted my red protection pouch and the thorn charm, both hanging around my neck, to draw the woman's attention that she was talking to someone in an "official" position.

"You must be joking," the old woman said again, and pulled out of her skirt pocket a small bundle which she held in my face. I recognized it immediately as a protection charm, a close replica of the one that Grandma also wore in the pocket of her dress. "This is not a children's game, this is serious and dangerous."

I opened my mouth to argue my position, but Grandma cut the discussion short:

"She's my granddaughter and apprentice. She has the gift of sight, same as myself. Tonight, she's helping us."

"Does she know…"

"Of course, she does," Grandma cut short the older lady, who – as I learned later – was the village's medicine woman, doftoroaie, and who could not deal with the situation, single-handed. Had my grandmother not been there, the doforoaie would have asked the medicine woman from the next village, for help.

"Of course, she knows what are we about to confront, what is expected from us, and what are the risks involved. Let's go at once," said Grandma.

My grandmother and I had arrived in the village two days before, at the invitation of Vica's parents. My parents were to arrive a few days later, just in time for Vica's engagement party. That night, we woke up to vigorous knocking at the door, and a woman's calling for Vica's mom to open. The two women who I just met, had given the short version of what my grandmother recognized as a malevolent fairy-being attempting to kidnap a baby. The village's medicine woman, having never dealt with a similar situation, felt lost. The sister of the young mother whose baby was threatened, had mentioned Grandma. I only then became fully aware to what extent Grandma's reputation preceded her. I felt proud to be her granddaughter, and believed that somehow her aura of fame would also resplend over me. On the other hand, the same fame she enjoyed put me under a lot of pressure. Since she introduced me as her granddaughter and apprentice, whatever I'd do or fail to do would reflect on Grandma too, I thought.

"Over here," said the younger woman, as she walked in front of us, to open the gate.

There was light shining in all the windows, and despite the time of the year, a thin curl of smoke came out of the chimney. We entered the house. Gas lanterns and candles burned everywhere. My first thought was to ask why don't they turn on the lights, because from what I knew, many inimical creatures –whether connected to fairies or not – were repelled not only by fire, but by bright light in general. However, I instantly remembered that the school, the mayor's office, and the medical dispensary were the only buildings in the village to have electricity. Glad that I didn't ask, I turned my focus on the task at hand. It was a pretty unsettling sight. Standing in the center of the room was the young mother, her eyes red from crying. She held the baby tight against her body, too afraid to lay it in the crib. The baby's father was prowling around with fire tongs in hand. When he saw Grandma, he leaped in her direction, grabbed her hand and kissed it, showing a degree of respect akin to veneration. I was speechless, breathless, and thoughtless.

"We thank you from the bottom of our hearts for helping us protect our little darling against...." The man's words faded, too afraid to say the name of the being that we were about to banish.

I reached inside the sleeve of my shirt and touched the wands. I had them both ready, blackthorn to banish and destroy, and fir to pacify, fortify, and grow. In the past weeks, I had practiced consistently, and learned so much about trees and fairy herbs, that I was sure I had become a specialist. That was until I entered that house and saw the panic-stricken faces. Feeling the wands restored my confidence. If Grandma trusted me enough to bring me along, I should also trust myself and my connections among fairies, whoever those might have been.

"It's almost midnight. We shall begin," said Grandma. Then she turned to the young mother: "By the time the sun's up two palms above the horizon, everything will be alright." She brought a chair for the mother. "You sit here, away from windows and doors. Hold your baby and don't put him down. If you need to rest your arms, even for one minute, you tell me, and I'll hold him." There was an outpour of gratitude in the young mother's eyes, that words could not convey.

Grandma went on, imparting instructions. She asked the man to circle the house three times, carrying around burning coals he would hold with the fire tongs. The local medicine woman was to walk with him and asperse with basil and holy water.

Grandma opened the bag she brought with her, and took out mugwort and the small ceramic dish she always used to burn herbs into. Next, she took out a jar with salt.

"Daniela, go ahead." I took out the blackthorn twig from my sleeve, and walked around the chair where the mother was sitting holding her baby asleep. I circled three times, each time asking Blackthorn itself and the Powers that I deemed to be our friends and allies, for protection. I had done everything as Grandma instructed me, as we left Vica's house. I eyed in her direction, hoping to see a sign of approval. But Grandma had no time for me. She lit up a bunch of mugwort, and while fumigating around the woman and throughout the room, she asked Mugwort for protection. Then she mixed salt with the mugwort ashes, and sprinkled a little bit of it over mother and baby. Then she scattered more around the room, especially by the door and windows.

We could hear the wind picking up making the fireplace flue whistle. The baby's father and the medicine woman finally came in. As they closed the door, a cup fell off the mantle and shattered. I felt my knees getting soft and my stomach quivering. Together with the younger woman, the one who accompanied the village's doftoroaie early on, Grandma prepared offerings for fairies: bread, milk, fresh water, a little cheese, all set up nicely on plates loaded on a tray. Covered with a beautifully embroidered white cloth. Once the tray was set on the table, Grandma began chanting in a soft melodious voice. She signaled me to join. Our voices united:

"Zânelor prea-bunelor..."

The ambers burst into flames. Something dropped outside with a loud thud. I instinctively laid my palm over the thorn charm that I wore and pressed it against my chest. The poor woman on the chair closed her eyes, and hunched over protecting the baby with her own body against an invisible danger. Her husband came near and hugged them both.

"Nothing to worry about," Grandma spoke, "at least not yet." Then she told the man to get up and check the candles and gas lanterns in the other room, making sure they were all lit up. There was something that I felt compelled to do, but I was also uneasy about leaving Grandma's side. I felt the nudging again, first as a whisper in my ear, then a tug at my sleeve. I was almost positive that I recognized the voice, and if that was who I thought it was, I knew that it would pester until I'd do what she asked me to. I left Grandma's side, taking a couple of tentative steps at first, as if checking that my legs with their rubber knees would actually support me. I reached the woman on the chair. I took off the charm that I had made from thorns, the one I deemed to be the most powerful protective amulet I had ever held, and gently put on the baby's belly. The woman stared at me inquisitively, afraid to speak so as not to wake up her little one.

"It's the most powerfully protective thing that I know of," I whispered close to her ear. "Please keep it."

"And you, what protections do you have?" asked Grandma when I returned to my place next to her.

"I have the wand, the pouch that we made together, and I believe I have a fairy guardian on duty." I paused, looked at her, and added: "I'm also standing next to you." Grandma made an effort to contain a smile.

Twice more we repeated our assigned tasks. Then, the dark blue began to pale, as if someone had watered down the celestial ink. Dawn was nearing. Another gust of wind rattled the door and made the old little house creak.

"It is that time" said Grandma, and we all went to the assigned tasks as planned, ready to carry on the ritual against the attempted baby abduction.

Grandma opened the door, and stood on the threshold facing outside. The mother, holding the child in her arms, stood behind

Grandma with her back toward the door. I handed Grandma the dish with water. Spilling the water in front of the door, she yelled: "The Powers of the Water shall drown you." Both herself and the medicine woman lit up torches which they waved while threatening the Old Woman of Woods, the fairy –being notorious for kidnapping babies – with burning. "The Powers of the Fire shall char you," Grandma shouted. She remained at her place while the other woman ran around outside the house carrying the torch and renewing the threats. Lastly, I gave Grandma the ax the baby's father had prepared. Grandma grabbed the ax with a power hard to imagine in an old lady. She knocked the threshold and the door jambs with it while threatening the Old Woman of the Woods with chopping her into pieces: "Shall you approach again, this ax will chop you into tiny pieces that the Power of Wind will scatter into all four corners of the world." A tall and crooked shadow swiftly crossed the courtyard, and vanished from sight. I felt my hair standing up.

"You shall leave this mother and her baby alone. You'll be smitten, drowned, burned and scattered, shall you dare show up again," Grandma continued, her voice firm, loud, and commanding. She took the ax, stepped outside and hit the ground with it. Then she brought the ax back inside and placed it under the baby's crib. The baby was finally laid in the crib. His mother hung above the crib the thorn charm together with a little cross that throughout the night, she clenched in her hand. Grandma said that until baptism, the baby should not be left alone, nor the ax removed from under the crib. The village's doftoroaie could take over from that point on.

We all went outside, except for the mother and baby, to conclude the ritual. Grandma invoked the powers of Water, Fire, and Wind asking them to keep away any malevolent being. Then we brought the offerings under a tree, for the spirits of the place and those goodly inclined among zâne whom we kindly asked to protect the house and all those who live in it.

Even in broad daylight, I still felt a little shaky. Sensing my emotions, Grandma reminded me that not all the fairies were benevolent, shiny beings, who would gather around to enjoy offerings we leave for them, imparting gifts and hugs in exchange.

"Do you understand what you are signing up for?" she asked. "I believe that you can still pull out."

"No. I'm not pulling out. I'll learn to be a fairy seer and a medicine woman like yourself."

"But why?"

"Because I can't see myself doing anything that doesn't have magic in it. Because I feel – I don't know how to explain this – a strange connection with the zâne, a desire to be around them."

"I see. Remember, this must be the call that comes from the heart. It is not about showing off. Your beliefs shall remain secret. People shall see only the results. Do not allow anyone to stick their nose into your private practice and your relationship with zâne."

I nodded, and took her by the hand. The women, who came to get us the night before, accompanied us back home. At Vica's house Grandma was hailed as a hero. As for myself, I was floating among the clouds.

Chapter 18

Marius' departure left a huge void. My best friend, the only kid with whom I could talk about everything crossing my mind at any moment, moved to another city, far, far away. In time, the stream of letters tapered off, first to a trickle, then to a mere greeting card on some holiday, and finally, to nothing at all. Then, the day came when my parents sat down with me and explained they were divorcing. Father made it clear that I wouldn't be staying with him; he was too busy and traveled a lot. It wasn't what he said, but the way he said it that broke my heart. Then, the argument exploded over what would happen with our house. I believed that I should have a say in the matter, but I was dismissed. I didn't go any farther than the threshold, though, just on the other side of the door, and there I sat, crouched on the cold slate, my ear glued to the polished wood surface. The more I heard, the more powerless and insignificant I felt, and life itself felt all the more unfair. Mother tried her best to talk Father out of selling the house, a decision he had taken single-mindedly. What I had just heard took me entirely by surprise. To add insult to injury, from listening to their argument, it came out that Father already had someone else in mind that he was planning to marry. Feeling betrayed on every single count, I ran outside, rage making my blood boil. I didn't give a damn about controlling it, only wanting to take it out on those who I believed looked the other way when they could have actually helped. Why did Grandma oppose doing any magic to keep my parents together? I didn't care about the explanations that she gave – binding is not the same as true love, that there's no magic that could make people wiser and more responsible, etc, etc. I didn't believe Grandma when she said that she'd done all that she could to help my parents' failing relationship. I did not want to believe Grandma when she said that magic cannot

156

and should not be used against people's conscious will and choice – I did not want to hear any of it, not when it came to my family and our home. Where were the fairies when I was asking for their help? No, I did not trust Grandma's explanation about fairies having different understanding of healthy or unhealthy relationships and to finding solutions for such problems. I yelled and cursed, kicked the ground and the stone by the blackthorn, as soon as I got there. I threw a rock toward the hedge when I perceived movement coming from that direction, and yanked myself from Grandma's arms when she tried to restrain me. I declared on the spot that fairies had miserably failed me, and I was mad at them. Grandma reminded me that fairies didn't owe anything to any of us. That being the case, I answered, I didn't owe them anything either.

A few days later the last load of furniture and household items left the house. A whole chunk of my life, a chapter ending on a note of deep disappointment and sadness, was packed up in the back of the truck that I watched moving away slowly.

Later that day, Grandma, Felix, and I, squeezed among luggage in the backseat of the cab, parked in front of the house. The driver got outside, leaned against the car door, and lit up a cigarette. We were waiting for Mother. Felix moved onto my lap. Sensing his agitation, I curled over and touched the fur on his back with my cheek. The gesture struck a chord with powerful resonance. In a flashback, I saw the young mother curling just like that over her baby. The night when I had stood at Grandma's side as her apprentice exploded in my memory. Then, I felt my soul slipping farther back to visit with an enthusiastic and flame-spitting kid who would burn down the world to become a witch and a fairy-seer; a kid gifted with a wand by fairies themselves after having been placed under a prohibition by the same fairies; a kid entitled enough to yell and hold fairies responsible for facts of life while that kid herself broke the prohibition, reading poker cards out of sheer curiosity; a kid who somehow felt above the rules. Suddenly, reality presented itself from a different angle. I felt embarrassed with myself. A sense of irreversible loss made my blood run cold. I slid Felix off my lap, climbed over the bag to my left, and scrambled out of the car.

Once my ritual space with the energy around it bubbling like a cup of Champagne, the area by the blackthorn felt cold and silent like a grave. It was wrapped in heavy stillness, as if life itself had abandoned the place. With its thorny branches stripped of leaves, the tree stood beneath the cloudy October sky, a black skeleton, a relic – no longer a sanctuary.

"I'm sorry," I whispered. My voice sounded eerie. Tears felt burning hot against my cold cheeks. "I'M SORRY!!"

Nothing moved. Even the clouds above stood frozen.

"Please…" I couldn't find my words. "Please come back," I finally articulated through sobs.

A little farther behind me, someone stepped on leaves, or so I thought. I turned around quickly enough to catch a glimpse of a tall, silvery silhouette flashing before my eyes before disappearing. I ran toward the woods.

"Wait! Come back! I'm sorry, I really am. How can I make up for what I did?"

The landing was harsh. The heels of my hands and the right knee were bleeding. I looked around my feet to see what had I tripped on, but I found nothing. My shoelaces were tied up neatly. There was no stone, twig, or anything else that could have caused me to fall. There was nothing else, just the bare ground of the familiar, well-trodden path that I knew probably better than the back of my own hand.

A gust of wind, then another one, swept over like waves tearing apart the fabric of stillness.

"One day, maybe…"

I wasn't sure about the words that I heard, whether the wind carried them from farther away, or I had just made them up in my head. I could not tell anything except that they resounded loud and clear at first, then faded until there was nothing but the wind whistling in my ears.

I walked back, and I found myself in front of the house in no time, unexplainably fast for how far into the woods I had gone; like it was not the same distance. Mother, who was just about to hand the house keys to one of the two people she was talking to, gasped at the sight of my bleeding hands and torn pants. I expected a scolding, resigned to the fact that I was fully deserving of it. Instead, Mom took me back inside and gently washed my face and my wounds. In the absence of anything else, she dressed my palms with paper napkins. There was gentleness in her every word and every gesture, there was sweetness and kindness, and so much consideration for what I felt and what prompted me to act the way I just did. No making fun, no denial or attempts to suppress my beliefs and experiences regarding fairies. A wall crumbled, and in the free, luminous space that it opened, our hearts reached toward each other, finally connecting.

"Mommy...uh, I'm here for you, ok?"

I realized that for the first time, I called Mother, mommy. I felt a little embarrassed, and tried to look away; an unnecessary precaution, because mommy was squeezing me so hard that I could barely breathe with my face buried in her jacket.

Grandma caught up with us.

"The timer on that cab is running, in case you have forgotten. I'll take it from here, the healing I mean, and by the time we reach our new home, she'll be much better."

Mom, Felix, and I squeezed among luggage in the backseat of the cab. Grandma had taken the front seat, near the driver. Their chatter, the music playing on the radio, and the warmth in the car made me sleepy.

"Come here," said my mother and pulled me closer so I could lay my head on her lap.

I did not know what lay ahead of me. I had no choice other than moving on. Or moving through. I had forfeited my relationship with the fairies, but somehow, miraculously, my mom found a way to connect with me. Happiness and sadness collided, and in canceling each other out, they left me suspended somewhere between dreams, worlds, hopes and fears, floating in a sea of non-sense.

"One day, I'll find out where I belong. And then, life will make sense again. One day."

Epilogue

The green is still pale on the branches. The puffy cloud just paused from its trip and now hangs right above me. Seen from this angle, it looks like a gigantic ball of white wool that got caught in the top of the maple. As I turn my head, the grass tickles my cheeks. Tiny yellow buttons peek at me through the green net that the grasses weave, as they dance with the breeze. The cloud travels again, blushing in the sunset. It's May Day Eve.

I prepare myself to journey. Until recently, May Day had lost its flavor. For years I've been wondering, learning, tackling paths, and ending up on tangents most of the time.

All along, there have been nudging, poking and prodding, all carrying a distinct signature that I deliberately ignored. But life can be weird, and consequently, that which I most arduously desired as a kid, now, in my adult years I have been pushing away. Instead, I have persistently clawed my way forward, on a spiritual path that I ultimately realized fitted me like a mitten – when a mitten is used to replace a sock.

I'm done with all that. I'm tired. No more swimming against the current. The time has come for me to surrender and listen to whoever needs to talk to me tonight. For once in my life, I am truly willing to listen.

With each breath I fall deeper within myself, floating, and dissolving into the monochromatic vastness behind my closed eyelids. Suddenly, it all goes dark. I believe that I'm still floating. When the darkness dissolves, I feel as if I am surrounded by very dense fog. I walk carefully, one step in front of the other, sensing the ground with my feet. As I advance, the fog thins out and I begin to discern the contours of trees. When the fog dissipates entirely, I find myself walking through a forest.

The place is vaguely familiar. I probably fell between sunsets, because here too, the sky turns red with the last fading daylight.

Something moves ahead, and from behind a tree a woman appears. As she draws near, I realize that she's at least one head taller than me, which makes her about seven feet high give or take a couple of inches. When I introduce myself, the smile on her face grows wider, her brown eyes glimmering with irony and mirth. The eyes...

I ask:

"Do I know you? Have we met before?"

No answer. The gaze is transfixing: I feel it simultaneously in my heart and in my head, and it hurts.

"Who are you? What's your name," I keep pressing while trying to breathe the pain away.

"I always wear white," comes the answer.

The past crashes onto my head like the Danube River at the Iron Gates[20]. I take the hand that she holds out for me, and I know there is no going back. Time collapses on itself: past, present, and future merge in a crucible and lay out in front of me the path I should be walking, a fairy path.

If you ask me, how does it feel to walk a Fairy-led path, I'll tell you honestly, that it is probably like nothing you have ever tried. On most days, it is inebriating wild. Sometimes it is an alternation of rock-climbing and rolling in flower-dotted green meadows. Sometimes it has the scent of ripe, sweet apples, and the crunch of autumn leaves, while other times it holds the dark and cold of graves and winter nights. It's not always pretty, not by human common standards anyway, and even when rapturous, it is never easy. In finding my path, I found myself, and I would not have it any other way.

Notes

1   At the time the events presented here occurred, 1974-
     1976, the Communist Regime was at the peak of its power
     in Romania. Public education was highly politicized.
     'Comrade' was the required way to address teachers. This
     was part of a fierce campaign to eliminate the use of words
     such as 'Madam' or 'Sir', considered bourgeois and unfit
     for use in Romania's "progressive" society.

2   I was clueless that writing such rain-checks to fairies was a
     no-no, and when I found out, it was a little too late.

3   *Fratii Jderi* by Mihail Sadoveanu, historical fiction,
     adventure.

4   Beginning in the early 70s, by the orders of the Communist
     Regime several churches were demolished or closed down,
     and priests forced into retirement.

5   Comrade Caran's career as an elementary school teacher
     ended a few months later. As a result of several parents
     complaining about her inadequacy as an educator, she was
     transferred to work in the school administration.

6   This is a relative paradox: while the policy was one of
     spiritual annihilation and forceful imposition of strict
     materialism, preservation of certain folk traditions
     was also important to the political regime. Many such
     traditions have historical roots that go far back to the time
     when the Romanian people and the Romanian language
     formed. Since the totalitarian regime in Romania was
     quite nationalist, the preservation of lore served a political
     agenda. To fit the purpose, lore and folk traditions were
     sanitized and presented strictly as the fossil reminder of a
     glorious and rich historical past.

7   It is hard to say that my upbringing was religious or
     not. While my family believed in the existence of a

supreme divinity, each family member had a different understanding of the Divine. My father was oscillating between agnosticism and atheism. My mother was a non-practicing Eastern Orthodox Christian. Grandmother was a practicing Eastern Orthodox Christian, but also believed in other beings which she called Powers who for some time I did not know who they were. I also knew that she strongly believed in zâne, the Romanian fairies. At the time in my life which is presented here, I did not know whether zâne and the Powers my grandmother was talking about were the same thing, whether there was only a partial overlap between the two, or if they were two separate things. My grandmother was very elusive whenever I tried to get a clear answer about who were the Powers that she mentioned so often.

8 Rusalii are very powerful fairies, not particularly fond of humans. They have their own holiday, the Feast of Rusalii that has been assimilated into Pentecost. Folk traditions, however, speak of them not only as inimical, but also as fairies with great healing powers which they use to help humans in certain circumstances. The queen of Rusalii, Irodia, Aradia, or Rusalia, protects ritual dancers, the Cālusari, who carry out healing and protective work during the week preceding the holiday of Rusalii. Since the Christian holiday of Pentecost shifts to align itself to Easter, the feast of Rusalii also changes date. However, it is very likely their eponymous holiday had once been connected to the movements of the Pleiades, whose apparition or disappearance from the night sky marked events in the agrarian calendar and the seasons' shifting.

9 An archaism, still in use, loosely translating as indigestion.

10 Artemisia absinthium (Artemisia vulgaris can substitute A. absinthium for protection and healing magic).

11 Valeriana officinalis.

12   Levisticum officinale (commonly used in cooking in many European countries).

13   Hyssopus officinalis.

14   Verbena hastata (Verbena officinalis is more commonly used, but my grandmother used blue vervain, V. hastata.)

15   Ritual folk dancers, who perform on the feast of Rusalii. Rusalii are fairies considered dangerous yet able to bestow healing on individuals and communities. The Cālusari / Kuh-loo-shari/ act under the patronage of Irodia/Aradia, the Queen of Rusalii.

16   Fairies who are celebrated on their eponymous holiday, June 23-24. They are benevolent, act friendly if encountered, and are generally goodly inclined toward humans. Sânziene are connected with magic, herbal healing, prosperity, love and passion. If offended they become very dangerous in their revenge. Their holiday has been assimilated into the holiday of St. John the Baptist.

17   The name given to practitioners of folk medicine in some parts of Romania.

18   "Fairies unmatched in kindness..." translated from Romanian.

19   Untranslatable, no linguistic equivalent, but can be approximated as fairy witch or fairy seer. In Romania the word witch is considered offensive by most people. Oftentimes, albeit not always, it is used pejoratively to denote malice, antiquated and awkward thinking and behavior. Magic workers and spiritual healers go by different names, such as doftoroaie and Soimancā.

20   The place where the Danube River cuts through the Carpathian Mountains. The eponymous power-plant, the largest in Romania, with its several turbines set in motion by a gigantic man-made waterfall, is located there.

Appendix A

Daniela's Little Book of Magic

In this section, I thought I would offer in a more organized format some of the spells and ritual material that I learned during my childhood years. There is no such claim that what is presented here is representative for the entire territory of modern Romania. Folk practices, especially the ones of fairy seers, vary greatly not only from community to community but from one practitioner to another. Since this section has been recreated from memory exclusively, it does not offer the entire content of the notebook mentioned in this narration.

The spells and charms listed here are NOT intended to replace any medical advice or medical care, or treatment but are offered for pure informational purposes. If you are dealing with an emergency, call emergency services.

Charm for Dry Cough

Supplies:
Water pitcher holding water, enough to fill a coffee cup (about 8 oz).
Matchbox, and 7 matches.
Ashtray.

The Work:
- Call onto the Powers one feels connected to (deities, fairy queens or kings, elves, healing spirits etc).
- Light up one match. While it burns, hold it over the water in the cup and say:

"As the water douses the flame, so this charm puts out the cough." Then douse the flame into the cup, and discard the burned match in the ashtray.

- Light up 6 more matches, one by one, and recite the charm over each burning match. Douse and discard.
- Say: "By the powers of the Fierce Ones, by the powers of the Holy Ones, by the powers of the Bright Ones I banish this disease. Cough shall vanish, as darkness vanishes with the rising of the morning sun. The new day shall find (name of person) healed from this ailment; may (he/she/they) rise up to vibrant health, fresh like spring flowers in the field."
- Make offerings to the Powers and spirit helpers.

Note:
Adapt the wording as you see fit, and call on the Powers that you work with in any way that suits you. Offerings can be fresh water, milk, butter, a little bit of food – anything that your tradition recommends.

Scattering Spell

Supplies:
A piece of paper. Optional, a pen.

The Work:
- Concentrate intensely on what you want to scatter: an obstacle, a vicious cycle of habits that prevents you from advancing, inconvenient people who control and block you, or something that you want to see falling apart. Choose only one thing to focus on. Optionally, you may write that specific thing on the piece of paper.
- Affirm that you are tearing apart, breaking, scattering the thing you have been focusing on, and tear apart the paper

into tiny pieces. Scatter the pieces on a flat surface, such as a table or the floor.

- Focus on how your life is without the obstacle that you scattered, and notice how that feels.
- Gather the pieces of paper and throw them into the trash can.

A Spell to Dispel Anger

Supplies:
Pen and paper.

The Work:
- Write down as much as you can about what or who makes you angry. Pour out your anger on paper.
- Tear the paper into small pieces.
- Drop the torn bits of paper in the toilet and flush it down the drain. You can also throw the pieces into the trash can, and then take the trash out.
- Throughout tearing the paper and then disposing of it, will your anger to be gone, so your mind can be clear and your heart be at peace.

Healing Charm Using a Poppet

Supplies:
A piece of cloth coming from a garment that was in touch with the skin of the person receiving the healing charm (like a piece of a t-shirt used for sleeping, for example).
Hair clippings.
Nails clippings.
Blessed water (made by the practitioner, water from a particular well or spring especially from a place that has healing

associations, holy water from church if befits the beliefs of practitioner and receiver, etc).
A thorn, toothpick, wood splinter, or needle (can be the same needle that you used for sewing).
Scissors.
Sewing thread and needle.
Pencil.

The Work:
- Invoke the help and guidance of those Powers and allies that you connect with whenever you do healing work.
- Draw twice the outline of a human body on the cloth: one is for the front and one is for the back. The two parts should match so you can assemble them to make a cloth doll.
- Cut out the two parts, then sew them together, as if you are making a rudimentary body-suit, leaving the top of the head open. Through the opening that you left at the top of the head, stuff in the hair, nail clippings, and bits from the remaining cloth until the limp "suit" becomes a little doll made of cloth. Sew the top opening. You can use the pencil to draw facial features and hair to increase the doll's resemblance to the receiver of the healing charm. The doll is known as a poppet and it is meant to embody the person benefiting from the charm.
- Name the poppet after the receiver of the healing charm: hold the poppet and say the name out loud, three times.
- Lay the poppet on a table, bed, altar, etc.
- Get the sharp thorn/toothpick/needle and gently run it along the poppet, from the head toward feet. The tool you are using does not point toward the doll, but runs parallel to the body, and the intention is to poke and disintegrate the disease that took hold of them. Move the tool along

the body following vertical lines, right and left form the median, covering the front. Then, turn the poppet face down and do the same for the back.

- If you are aware of a specific area in the body that is affected, insist on working on it; move the sharp tool repeatedly through that spot, parallel to the body and not pointing toward it.
- For as long as you do this, hold the person that you work for in loving awareness, willing the ailment to disintegrate and the receiver to feel relief.
- When you get the sense that the procedure is complete, sprinkle water over the poppet. Use any prayer or healing blessing that you know, or make up one of your own, extempore.
- Use the sharp object to threaten the disease with total annihilation by the Powers whose help you enlisted if it ever dares to be upset again (...name of the receiver...)
- Close the session by giving thanks to the Powers who assisted you.
- You may have to repeat the charm, so keep the doll safe from one session to the next.
- When the whole cycle has ended, dismantle the poppet.
- Bury the dismantled popped at the root of a tree, intending for the (....name of receiver...) to grow strong and healthy as the mighty tree, while the disease shall be buried and decompose, as the cloth decomposes in the soil.

Note:

Adapt the charm as you see fit. If you are familiar with other healing techniques, using plants and crystals, you can integrate these into the sessions. It is always good to make offerings to the Powers, who provide assistance and protection. Offerings can be fresh water, milk, butter, a little bit of food – anything that your tradition recommends.

Making Blessing Water

Supplies:
Candle preferably white, but any color you prefer should be fine.
Lighter or matches.
Bottle with water (water from melting snow, rainwater, water from a specific well or spring, holy water from church, if this is something the practitioner resonates with, etc)
Empty jar, 16 or 32 oz, or larger if you wish, depending on how much blessing water you are going to make.
Dried herbs: Basil, Sage, Lavender.

- Basil, *Ocimum basilicum*, traditionally used in Romanian folk tradition and religious practices to banish negative, disruptive entities, or simply refresh the energy of a space. It also propitiates the presence of friendly entities, spirit guides and allies.
- Sage, *Salvia officinalis*, commonly used in Romanian folk medicine to propitiate calm and banish negative, aggressive energies, such as anger. Same as Basil, it also invites the presence of friendly entities, spirit guides and allies.
- Lavender, *Lavandula angustifolia*, is used more in the western parts of Romania as part of folk remedies. Lavender is calming in the same way sage is, but with a more refreshing and upbeat feel to it. It dissolves the bad, heavy feeling that permeates a space where an argument took place or where something bad happened.
- (Use herbs that you feel a primary connection with, and which you would associate with blessing a space and elevating its energy. You can add more than three herbs if you wish, or use just one. In making blessing water, keep in mind who are your spirit allies, who are your allies in

171

general, what deity, or fairies do you connect with: use herbs that agree with these.)

A stone that is meaningful to you and the characteristics of which are synergistic to the blessing water that you make. For example, my Grandmother used a bit of black granite, because: "...granite shall lend to this water something that you need: strength and stability. You can't live with your head in the clouds unless you have your feet very firmly planted on the ground. You want to be calm and patient, enduring like granite itself, and not be easily tossed and turned around by spirits, good or bad, or feelings, good or bad." While I personally favor bits of rock that are found during hikes or on the beach, you may prefer crystals.

The Work:
- Light up the candle. Stand at the center of the space and hold the candle, focusing on the work you intend to do. (Make sure you do not drip wax on yourself or rugs; make sure you wear fitted clothes that will not drag over the flame and catch fire!)
- Set up sacred space following the directions below or in any way that you choose based on your personal practice.
- Turn East, and say, "To the Powers in the Rising Sun!" (You may explicitly name Powers that you do associate with this direction, with the rising sun, making the call as specific or generic as you like.)
- Turn South, and say, "To the Powers of Midday!" (You may explicitly name Powers that you do associate with this direction, with the sun's position in the middle of the day, making the call as specific or generic as you like.)
- Turn West and say, "To the Powers in the Setting Sun!" (You may explicitly name Powers that you do associate with this direction, with the sunset, making the call as specific or generic as you like.)

- Turn North, and say, "To the Powers of Midnight!" (You may explicitly name Powers that you do associate with midnight, making the call as specific or generic as you like.)
- Turn again to face the starting point, lift the candle a little higher, and say, "To the Powers in the Sky Above," (You may explicitly name Powers that you do associate with the Sky or with the Above, making the call as specific or generic as you like.)
- Bow slightly to lower the candle, and say, "To the Powers in the Earth Below". (You may explicitly name Powers that you do associate with the Earth, Underworld, or with the Below, making the call as specific or generic as you like.)
- Bring the candle in front of yourself. Feel that you are at the center of all directions intersecting. Call onto your spirit allies, all those whose help you wish to enlist, in preparing the blessing water.
- Pause. Sense how the space feels, and how you feel. Place the candle somewhere safe.
- Open the small jar.
- Get a pinch of Basil. Now hold it in your palms. Close your eyes and briefly meditate on its properties, then ask Basil to lend its power to the blessing water that you are making. Put it in the jar.
- Get a pinch of Sage. Now hold it in your palms. Close your eyes and briefly meditate on its properties, then ask Sage to lend its power to the blessing water that you are making. Put it in the jar.
- Get a pinch of Lavender. Now hold it in your palms. Close the eyes and briefly meditate on its properties, then ask Lavender to lend its power to the blessing water that you are making. Put it in the jar.
- Pick up the stone. Hold it in your palms. Close your eyes and briefly meditate on its properties, then ask (...name

of the stone/crystal...) to lend its power to the blessing water that you are making. Put it in the jar on top of the herbs.

- Hold the bottle with water. Close your eyes and briefly meditate on its properties. If there is any association with any location, nature spirit, fairy being, deity, saint, etc, then ask the water to lend its power to the blessing mixture that you are making. Pour it in the jar. Add some alcohol to prevent the herbs from rotting, and later, the herb-infused water from fermenting. Screw the cap on.

- To close the ritual, take the candle, raise it slightly, and thank all the Powers that assisted you in the ritual, collectively.

- Walk around the space clockwise (if you first turned counterclockwise), and intend the energy of the space to become energetically neutral again and suited for daily, non-ritual activities.

- Place the jar on the windowsill where it will benefit from exposure to both sunlight and moonlight, for three days. You can time the preparation with the phases of the moon. Prepare the water on the day preceding the first night of the full moon (or on that very night, if you prefer). Your water and herbs will sit in the full moon light for three nights, and you can strain it on the following day.

- After three days, strain the water and keep it in a bottle. Use for aspersing spaces that you want to bless, tools, clothing garments. You can use it for yourself, family members, pets by aspersing onto them.

- Dispose of the herbs respectfully. You can put them in compost or leave them somewhere outside on the ground.

- You can reuse the rock/crystal for any other charm you wish to do in the future.

Note:

Notice that in setting sacred space, I mentioned turning from East to South to West to North, which is counterclockwise. The reason for this is the belief that in turning counterclockwise, one opens the gates to Fairy. (I work specifically in partnership with fairies; you may have to adapt the setting of sacred space to fit your tradition, training, and personal preferences.) My reason for setting up the space this way is twofold: opening the portal for my Fairy allies to come in, and set up a space which I deem sacred where only the energies and entities that are supportive of my intent for the work will be able to enter.

Under no circumstance drink from the water that you have prepared, and do not use it for gargling, wash your eyes, or put it in your ears. If you are dealing with a medical condition, call your doctor.

Spell to Relieve Indigestion

Supplies:
Bucket, in case someone throws up.
Medium size basin or kitchen bowl.
Towel.
Pitcher with about 6 cups of water in it.
Small fireproof dish to burn things into.
Matches.
Small bundle of pig hair (a few hairs would suffice) tied with red thread. In case there is no way to procure pig's hair, replace it with a small piece of dried wormwood and a few leaves of peppermint/mint, tied with red thread.
Sprig of basil, fresh or dry.

The Work:
- Have the afflicted person lay down or sit comfortably.

- Light up the tiny bundle of hair, (or herbs) put it in the bowl and make it smolder.
- While smoldering, circle the ailing person 3-5 several times wafting smoke toward them. Think of the indigestion as a personified energy, and order it to leave.
- Pour a little water in the basin: dip the fingertips and massage the receiver's right forearm, using upward-going strokes, from wrist toward the crease of the elbow.
- While massaging, say this charm or something similar of your own making:

"Go away, Indigestion/Malaise!
You are unwanted,
You are cursed,
I am nagging and poking you,
and squeezing you out of this belly and out of this body
Out of these legs,
And out of these arms,
So (...Name...) shall remain
Clean and fresh like flowers in the field,
Tall and vigorous like a fir tree."

- Repeat 3 times while massaging the right forearm.
- Repeat 3 times while massaging the left forearm.
- Repeat 3 times while massaging both temples simultaneously.
- Spit (pretend, by just making the noise and the gesture) over the receiver's head, as if aiming at someone standing behind them, thinking that you are banishing the disease through the act of ritual use of spitting (gesture).
- Have the person stand up and move to a different chair or couch.
- Pour some water in the basin and rinse hands.
- Throw into the toilet and flush, or if throwing outside,

warn any potential fairy bystander by announcing, "Water is coming!"

- Pour fresh water into the basin. Dip the basil sprig and asperse the place where healing took place: the place where the receiver was seated and the space around.
- Throw the water in the same way as before.
- Thank Basil for assistance in cleansing and protecting the space, and dispose of the sprig respectfully (compost, leave outside by a tree, in a flowerbed, etc).

Simple Warding Using a Wood Wand

Supplies:
Wood wand; it can be a plain twig.

The Work:
- Stand at the center of the space that you want to ward. Focus on what you seek to accomplish, namely, to create a barrier to enclose the space you wish to ward. Make it clear that your intent is to keep out only the entities and energies that are inimical. Be specific about who you want to allow inside your ward.
- Hold the wand in your dominant hand, and point it to the periphery of the space. Turn around, and visualize energy streaming from the tip of the wand and creating a boundary that encloses the space. You can turn around once or three times, visualizing how the boundary grows first into a wall, and how then it becomes an enclosure. Make the enclosure feel spacious and luminous.
- Put the wand away, and if necessary, renew the warding every week, month, or season, depending on the situation.
- You may use this type of warding independently or in addition to other space protection techniques.

Note:
Ward selectively. Make sure that the wand you are using is made of wood that agrees with your spirit allies and it is concordant at least to some extent to the lore associated with them. If you know your spirit ally, fairy, for example, is averse to rowan, then don't use a rowan wand for warding. Try oak, ash, or ebony instead.

Herbal Charm to Banish Malevolent Spirits

Supplies:
One pinch of the following herbs, dry or fresh:

Mugwort. Artemisia absinthium (Artemisia vulgaris can substitute A. absinthium for protection and healing magic)
Valerian. Valeriana officinalis
Lovage. Levisticum officinale
Hyssop. Hyssopus officinalis
Vervain. Verbena hastata or Verbena officinalis
You can replace one or several herbs based on the knowledge you have and tradition you are trained in. Most importantly, make sure that none of the herbs that you use conflicts with the preferences of your spirit allies because you do not want to drive those away. Study the lore of the pantheons/cultures that make up the foundation of your spiritual practice, and corroborate those sources with your own personal experience derived from meditation or otherwise.

Small cloth pouch (or a square piece of cloth approximately 5x5 in, red thread, and scissors)

The Work:
- Set up sacred space (you may simply light up a candle and ask your spirit allies to assist you).

- Get your cloth pouch handy; or lay the piece of cloth on a flat surface.
- Get each herb, keep it between your palms, focus on its protective qualities, and ask it to lend its energies to your protection charm. Put the herb in the pouch, or place it at the center of the cloth.
- After adding the last herb to the pouch, close it. If you are using a piece of cloth instead of a pouch, gather the corners to make a bundle, and tie it with red thread; use scissors to trim the corners and the thread.
- Hold the pouch between your palms: ask the herbs to protect you against (...list what kind of energy do you need to be protected against...) during sleep.
- Place the pouch/bundle under the pillow. You can make an additional one to carry around in the bag or pocket, or wear them around your neck, as you would do with any protective amulet.

Appendix B

Resources

As an autobiography, this book per se does not draw from any other book or written source that could be indicated in a bibliography section. However, I wish to give readers an integrated view by placing personal experiences into cultural context. To this avail, I did my best to find sources that document folk traditions and the work of folk healers in Romanian culture. Below is a list of resources that offers those interested more information on Romanian indigenous practices on a broader level.

Books:

Eliade, Mircea, *Occultism, Witchcraft, and Cultural Fashions: Essays in Comparative Religions*, 1976

Ghinoiu, Ion, *Folk Almanac*, 2005

Ispirescu, Petre, *Romanian Folktales*, 2016

Kligman, Gail, *Cālus, Symbolic Transformation in Romanian Ritual*, 1981

Mawr, Elisabeth B., *Roumanian Fairy Tales and Legends*, 1861; reprinted Columbia
Press, 2021

Spariosu, Mihai I and Dezsö, Benedek, *Ghosts, Vampires, and Werewolves. Eerie Tales from Transylvania*, 1994

Simina, Daniela, *Where Fairies Meet: Parallels between Irish and Romanian Fairy Traditions*, 2023

Talos, Ion *Petit Dictionaire de Mythologie Popular Roumaine*, French translation by Anneliese and Claude Lecouteux, 2002

Research Papers and Articles:

Pócs, Éva, "Small Gods, Small Demons: Remnants of an Archaic Fairy Cult in Central and South-Eastern Europe", 2018

Vivod, Maria, "The Fairy Seers of Eastern Serbia: Seeing Fairies-Speaking through Trance", 2018

About the Author

Daniela Simina grew up in Romania, immersed in the rich local fairy lore. From a very young age, she apprenticed with her grandmother, a fairy seer and medicine woman. Walking in her grandmother's footsteps, she became a medicine woman and fairy witch. Daniela is passionate about researching Irish, Romanian, and Germanic/Norse fairy folklore and traditions which are the foundation for her personal spiritual practice. She continues to study under the guidance of scholars who are invested in preserving the historical and folkloric heritage within these cultures. In addition to writing and researching, Daniela Simina teaches classes on energy healing and various esoteric subjects revolving around fairies.

Titles by the same author:

Where Fairies Meet: Parallels between Irish and Romanian Fairy Traditions, the first study that brings side-by-side Irish and Romanian fairy traditions, gives scholars, lay people, and spiritual seekers access to an everlasting repository of wisdom encapsulated in the fairy lore and anecdotal accounts from past and present. Throughout the book, the parallelism between the two cultures is explored in a way that invites reader's pondering over the reality behind fairy phenomena.

From the Author:

Thank you for purchasing *A Fairy Path*. My sincere hope is that you found this book to be useful, and that you enjoyed reading it as much as I did creating it. If you have a few moments, please feel free to add your review of the book to your favorite online site; I would be immensely grateful. Also, if you would like to connect with other books and events that I have coming in the near future, please visit my blog https://whispersinthetwilight. blogspot.com/, website https://siminayoga.com, and Simina Yoga Facebook page, for news on upcoming works and recent blog posts.

Sincerely, Daniela Simina

You might also like

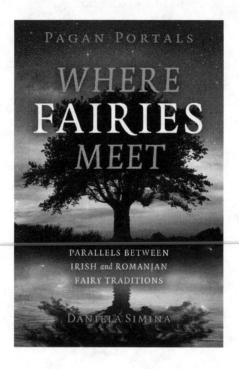

Where Fairies Meet: Parallels Between Irish and Romanian
Fairy Traditions Daniela Simina

978-1-80341-019-7 (Paperback
978-1-80341-230-6 (e-book)

**MOON
BOOKS**

MOON BOOKS
PAGANISM & SHAMANISM

What is Paganism? A religion, a spirituality, an alternative
belief system, nature worship? You can fi nd support for
all these definitions (and many more) in dictionaries,
encyclopaedias, and text books of religion, but subscribe to
any one and the truth will evade you. Above all Paganism is
a creative pursuit, an encounter with reality, an exploration
of meaning and an expression of the soul. Druids, Heathens,
Wiccans and others, all contribute their insights and
literary riches to the Pagan tradition. Moon Books invites
you to begin or to deepen your own encounter, right here,
right now.

If you have enjoyed this book, why not tell other readers by
posting a review on your preferred book site.

Readers of ebooks can buy or view any of these bestsellers by clicking on the live link in the title. Most titles are published in paperback and as an ebook. Paperbacks are available in traditional bookshops. Both print and ebook formats are available online.

Find more titles and sign up to our readers' newsletter
http://www.johnhuntpublishing.com/paganism

Follow us on Facebook
https://www.facebook.com/MoonBooks

Follow us on Instagram
https://www.instagram.com/moonbooksjhp/

Follow us on Twitter
https://twitter.com/MoonBooksJHP

Follow us on TikTok
https://www.tiktok.com/@moonbooksjhp